C000007282

The Relationship Revolution

The Relationship Revolution

CLOSING THE CUSTOMER PROMISE GAP

Larry Hochman

A John Wiley and Sons, Ltd, Publication

To Eric, who made my life complete

Contents

Acknowledgements

To the many people who have lent their support and encouragement through the years, a simple thank you. They include: Judy and Brian Robson, Alan Deller, Mike Pegg, Simon and Anita Wood, Andrea Burton, Colin Marshall, Elizabeth Gudonis, Dr Stan Maklan, Jacqueline Smith, John Wyman, Jane and Eric Bischoff, June Sebley, Mia and Francois Touzin, Scott and Robin Gustlin, the O'Halleran family, Brendan Barns, Santiago Zapata, Denise Bacci, Francesca Scarpa, Francesco Lorenzoni, Martin Gould, Larry Dumont, Sharon Bowler, CSA Consultants Worldwide, Amanda Mackenzie, Steve Hurst, Nick Duxbury, Cosimo Turroturro, Christina Wood, Mariam Mohamed, Sheldon and Trudy Wiseman, John O'Regan, Zar Nicholson, Sue Moore, Enrique Vessuri, Bill George, Georgie and Paul Johnson, my brilliant editor at John Wiley & Sons Ellen Hallsworth…and of course Eric.

'In the eyes of the wise, the moment
is better than the entire world'

Imad al-Hasain, sixteenth century Persian poet

Introduction

Customers for Life...Priceless!

The urgency of the economic moment is clear. No one person alone has all the answers. This recession has created a massive disruption in the way that organisations relate to the people they serve, and amplified customers' sense of being taken for granted at a time when everyone is cynical, angry and full of anxiety. You, as a business leader, are now faced with one commercial fact of life: the ability to build and maintain successful customer relationships, during and after the recession, is the key to the survival of your business. This is where Unique Value has always been created, value that can seldom, if ever, be replicated by any competitor. The companies that emerge from the fear and confusion of recession will be the ones which have both the *clarity* and the *confidence* to focus on customer relationships to make their businesses unique; to create Value for Life. This should be your quest. Indeed, the quest of this book is to help you focus better on this reality, and to point out the grave danger if you fail to do so at this fragile time of recovery.

We live in an era where loyalty programmes have become a commodity, an era where trust and confidence in business leadership has collapsed, an era where there are no monopolies, an era where customer choice is rampant, an era where taking for granted even one single customer is a huge risk. We live in an era where, owing to enabling technology, customers are now in control forever, at the touch of their computer keyboards able to punish you and potentially destroy what you have spent years building.

For years, customers have been growing increasingly cynical about the gap that exists between the promises that companies make to them and the realities of what is actually delivered. Far from just being cynical, today's consumers actually believe that companies (and governments) are lying to them. Tough times have changed what they value, who they trust, how and what they wish to purchase, and hardened their determination to punish. Let down, exhausted, feeling out of control, they are seeking the stability of business relationships where companies feel loyal to *them*, where small kindnesses are practised, where recognition is commonplace, where simplicity and speed are the rule, not the exception. We are now entering the post-recession era. This brings with it enormous challenges and dangers. The biggest challenge, of course, is the continued survival of your business. The expression 'a crisis is a terrible thing to waste' has never been more true. All companies need to comprehensively review their level of obsession with customers, making necessary strategic and structural changes in order to do the following things.

You must *get closer* to customers to understand what people really need *right now* (not what they needed five years ago, two years ago or even last year). You must then *get smarter* about what is being delivered based on current knowledge, not guesses or history. Finally, you must 'Get Ready' to urgently focus the entire organisation on customer relationships in the post-recession era to guarantee continued survival.

The crucial thing which all companies must understand is that almost everything in your business can be replicated. Competing on price isn't hard – anyone can do it, today, tomorrow, as you're reading this sentence. Competing on product is easy, too – there are people in China and India waiting to take any innovation to pieces and put it back together again, faster, better and cheaper.

The only things that can't be replicated are the relationships you have with your customers. The one-to-one interactions that you build up with them, over days, weeks, months and years, are truly unique and truly earned. They cannot simply be 'Googled'. It is within these relationships that Unique Value in your company is created. These relationships are the key to sustainable business success.

Like all relationships, however, the relationships that you have with your customers must be based on *trust that is earned*. Think of the closest, most important relationship in your own personal life – most likely this will be the relationship you have with your husband, wife, partner or lover. Those

The ability to build and maintain customer relationships is the key to the survival of your business

of you who have experienced the collapse of trust in a marriage will know this hard truth: the things that made that personal relationship uniquely valuable are hard to recover. Often the relationship will never recover. Faced with exactly this kind of collapse in many of their business relationships owing to the recession, if they no longer trust you, customers will dump you faster than you ever imagined possible. They are likely to demand unprecedented levels of transparency, openness, accountability, honesty and delivery in order to trust you in the future. The revolution is their revolution, and the ease with which they can walk away from you, never tell you why, instead tell 10,000 others in their online community about how you lost their trust – is today's post-recession reality.

You can't buy word-of-mouth recommendation or reputation

Customer relationships are uniquely important and valuable because they are so very fragile. Again, like your personal relationships, they can take years to work on, develop and grow. And yet, overnight, by just one bad mistake, one small indication that rather than valuing your customers you have contempt for them, or take them for granted, or lied to them, or over-promised and under-delivered, a customer might walk away and *never* return.

Several years ago, Customer Relationship Management (CRM) software was heralded as a new dawn for business, a way in which important commercial relationships could be strengthened and maintained by the collection of information, believing this was the road to perfecting the art of customer loyalty. Companies all over the world invested thousands, and sometimes even millions, installing software to track and manage customers. Looking back, it's hard to assert that this made any difference at all to the way that customers felt about the companies they interacted with, or to levels of customer loyalty. Indeed, it may even have been corrosive to both. The belief that loyalty could be sustained by the collection of information led to customers being commoditised. The truth is that relationships are not that mechanical: that's what makes them scary and wonderful. There's no way to 'de-risk' relationships through software, which was the basic, if unspoken, promise of CRM. All you can do is make sure that everyone in your company genuinely understands how important relationships are, fully appreciates how they link to the bottom line, and works at strengthening them all the time no matter what their job is. Many have been led to believe that everything can be measured and quantified. A Customer for Life is such a valuable thing that he or she is genuinely priceless.

The Relationship Revolution is the name I give to the process of change that now engulfs us, and to which all businesses will have to adapt if they are to survive. This revolution will take several different forms, and new ways of doing business and thinking about customers will emerge from it. One of the most important aspects of the revolution is the exponential power customers now have to communicate, participate and collaborate. These are powerful tools which can be used to either reward or punish you depending on your ability to deliver on your promises.

Much has been written about how the new social networks will change the way that products are marketed. Much less has been written about the implications that this has for the survival of your business. In a world where customers are connected and can organise in huge numbers at very short notice, they are in fact forming Customer Unions, more instrumental than Trade Unions ever were to the commercial success of your business. We have yet fully to understand the implications of this. It is likely, though, that these fleeting, ephemeral, and yet ferociously influential Customer Unions may well have effects on business in the post-recession era that will be *the* dominant factor in the determination of commercial success – or failure. Word of mouth and reputation are now far, far more important than advertising. The terrifying and exciting thing is that, unlike advertising, you can't buy word of mouth. You can't pay astronomical fees to an agency to create and manage a reputation for you in the turmoil of the Relationship Revolution. You need to work at these in every interaction, every single day.

Again and again, when people are asked who they most trust to recommend a product or service to them, they come up with the same answer: 'someone like me'.[1] That's not you as a business leader, nor your marketing team, nor your advertising partner. It's their neighbours, their family, their work colleagues, the other members of their online

---

1 Edelman Trust Barometer, 2006

community; their companions in the Customer Union. Your customers want you to tell the truth, they want you to deliver on your promises, they want their lives made less rather than more complicated, they want service and information at the speed of *life*, their life, made easier by the products and services you offer. They want someone to say 'I'm sorry' and mean it when something goes wrong.

Customer relationships are not the only relationships that matter in business. In fact, relationships are at the heart of everything that happens in commercial life. Customer relationships may be the *sine qua non*, life or death issue, but there are many other relationships of huge commercial significance. These are your relationships with colleagues, business partners, investors, competitors, media, and sometimes with the government. The success or failure of these relationships is determined, like all others, by the levels of trust established and maintained, and they will all have a demonstrable effect on your ability to attract and retain customers and create Unique Value in your business.

Size has never mattered less. In the post-recession era, it's all about focus

Corporate culture is governed today by a kind of 'emotional contagion'. If everyone in a company is focused on ethics, values, and customers, it infuses right to the heart of what you do. And yet the opposite is also true – if employees don't understand the kind of trust and confidence that underpin a meaningful relationship, if the media and your investors mistrust the line you try to spin, it's very hard for customers to feel any differently. Ethics do not belong in the ghetto of a single department or director; they are the keystone of all responsible business and, therefore, part of every single employee's job description. Size has never mattered less. In the post-recession era, it's all about *focus*. In the chapters that follow, I will focus on what went wrong in the way that businesses have related to customers, and what Unique Value really looks like today. I want to help you build up a picture of what this revolution looks like, what it means for you, and how it will help your business grow, succeed and indeed survive. I want this book to give you a *vision* of what a better commercial future can look like and, finally, to inspire you with the *courage* you need to achieve this; to live the Relationship Revolution every day in your business life.

The urgency of the economic moment is clear

My global reputation has been built on understanding the role that customer relationships play in business success or failure, and trying to communicate this to others. I've travelled to more than 60 different countries and given nearly 500 speeches in the past twelve years. I think I have the best job in the world. I've been able to learn about how this fact of commercial life transcends cultures and industries to lie at the very heart of business in every industry, everywhere in the world – relationships are a universal truth. Prior to that, I was a member of senior management teams at British Airways and the loyalty management company Airmiles, working in both New York and London. At British Airways, I helped to create and then helped to manage what is judged by many as the most successful corporate training programme ever conducted in Europe, a programme called Winning for Customers, attended by over 55,000 BA staff. As a result, pilots, cabin crew, cooks, IT experts, HR administrators, engineers, company directors and others came together every day for a period of three years in cross-functional groups of 100. The goal was for them to understand better that customers lay at the very heart of BA's success and profitability, that to gain customer loyalty was the job of every single person, and that to lay claim to our status as 'the world's favourite airline' (which at that time was the truth!), everyone had to take responsibility to live these values every day. At Airmiles, I became Director of Customer Service and then, separately, Director of People and Culture. I was the first person in any European company to ever have this role and title, created in recognition that the same sense of urgency was required to focus on internal *and* external relationships, and the success of the business was dependent on getting both right.

I've seen for myself the kind of rewards that come from properly understanding the importance of relationships and getting them right. They have always mattered, but today they matter more than ever. The urgency of the economic moment is clear, and there is such beauty in the simplicity of it. The importance of the issue is irrefutable. The thing you have to do is act.

To paraphrase Bill Clinton, 'it's the customer, stupid'. And as the Madison Avenue advertising legend David Ogilvy once famously said: 'The customer isn't a moron. She is your wife! Don't lie to her and do not insult her intelligence.'

Achieving this closeness to your customer is the greatest investment you can ever make. It is where your Unique Value as a company is created and maintained. It is at the heart of your commercial success – or failure. Be part of the revolution. The time is now.

Chapter 1

The Search for Unique Value

Today, everyone is searching for value. *Everyone!* That is the biggest, harshest, most challenging reality of the post-recession era through which we are all now living. Some people are going to Wal-Mart and McDonald's for the very first time. Some are trading down from private jets to first class, from first class to business class, and from business class to economy. Others are choosing not to travel at all. Value is at the forefront of every consumer's mind, at every end of the value chain. Every purchase, every decision, is made with that single idea looming large. This doesn't just mean that people are spending less. It's true that many people are, but what almost everyone is doing is trying to do more with less. In the messy aftermath of global recession, when people do spend money, they will want to feel they have achieved value in doing so. The success or failure of every business at this crucial moment in time depends on understanding this notion of value as never before. Hope is not a strategy. So you'd best have a plan.

Do not, however, fall into the trap of confusing value with price. To do this is to pursue the strategic equivalent of a commercial dead end. Anyone can beat you on price, more or less any time. Price is far too simple to be the lodestar of success or failure. We live in a hyperglobalised world, a world in which labour and intellectual property seem to move at the speed of light. There is, and always will be, someone out there who is able to do what you do, more or less, more cheaply than you can. Manufacturing, and now even services,

flit around the globe endlessly, landing in a cheaper place
and then leaving it again as their presence has made it more
expensive. Price wars are endless and are likely to be bloody.
Once you are sucked into the vortex of competing solely
on price, you must realise that you're unlikely to win at all.
Most likely, you will end up being a big loser. If you rely
entirely on price, you could soon become a commodity. The
end result will be that you lose power to control pricing, as
you'll be following, not leading. What are the long-term consequences of this? What will this do to
the long-term value of your company?
Be honest with yourself – how close
are you to having this happen? How
can you avoid it?

Hope is not a strategy

Price is not the only trap into which the pressures of a
recession may lead you. Clearly, everyone reading this book
will have been focused on cutting costs, even cutting staff, as
a result of this recession. It's likely that you have been looking
at all expenditures and thinking in cold, hard terms about
how essential they really are, and what the impact of doing
without them would be. Your budgets for the year ahead
are probably displaying a distinctly downward trend. Yet, in
addition to the threat of becoming a commodity, there is another, perhaps even greater, problem linked to cutting costs.
How do you cut costs without cutting your own throat? The
demands of your customers are increasing, not decreasing,

as a result of the recession. Cutting back and sitting tight is not an easy way out.

Please don't think, either, that having a superior product will give you enough value to stay safe. As a competitive strategy, great products may not be as deadly simple as low prices, but they are nearly as replicable. If you decide to rely on your product, at the expense of price and relationships, you are likely to see all your hard work overtaken and your unique advantage disappear within a matter of months, if not weeks. The global marketplace is littered with the wreckage of businesses which fell victim to 'second mover advantage'. Companies who relied heavily on their products and forgot that others out there were able to take advantage of their research and development, without the costs, were never able to recover from this. Look at Atari. They were first to market with a gaming machine. Hot on their heels, however, followed Nintendo. Today, decades later, with the Wii, Nintendo has dominated and changed the face of computer games. Who's got an Atari now? With a truly great product, it's easy to win in the short term. The best products create new markets, or new standards in existing markets. But almost as soon as they arrive, they can be, indeed they will be, imitated. No successful company is able to compete on product alone.

To compete solely on product, cost, or price in the post-recession era is to build your house on sand. What marks out the companies that have succeeded in the recent past, a trend which will only intensify in a more difficult future, is that they possess that genuine commercial gold dust: *Unique Value*. This is value which cannot be copied or imitated, as easily, if ever, by any competitor. This Unique Value resides in the relationship that you have with your customers, and they with you. These customer relationships, the personal one-to-one interactions that people have with your company, built up over time and based on trust, have a truly immense impact on their brand loyalty – and, ultimately, on your bottom line. These relationships are not like one-night stands. They exist over long periods of time. They go beyond any loyalty card or scheme which, as we've discussed earlier, have now themselves become a commodity. In a service economy, long-term, one-to-one relationships are the only thing that you can aspire to do better than the next person. Such relationships will be the dominant factor determining success in the post-recession era. They not only create Unique Value, they create Value for Life. That is the core premise of this book.

Unique Value cannot be easily quantified, but it must be understood. Unique Value consists of understanding, not just guessing, what your customers want, and then consistently giving it to them better than they could ever have known they wanted it. The mission of this book is to help you identify where the Unique Value is in your company.

Here's an interesting thought experiment, which illuminates quite well the importance of Unique Value and where it lies. If, God forbid, you went under a bus tomorrow, you probably know exactly who would care: your partner, your friends, your parents, your kids, your neighbours. In your personal relationships, it's almost certainly a lot easier. But what if your company went under the same bus? Imagine that your business disappeared overnight. Plenty have in recent years, and many more are likely to in the years to come. Who would really miss it? Who would come to your corporate funeral? Your customers, your supplier, your competitors? Why would they be there?

The premise of this book is that corporate success is founded on relationships that are just as deep and take just as much work as the ones in your personal life. This is a kind of corporate version of the film *It's a Wonderful Life*. Would your customers really feel that you were irreplaceable in their lives? Would your suppliers think they had lost a company which they really enjoyed trading with? Would your employees feel that they had lost not just a job, but also the chance to be part of something really special, something that made a difference? Would the media bemoan the loss of a company that had made your particular industry just that bit more interesting or exciting? Think hard about this; even ask the people around you. Once you have isolated the people who would care if your company ceased to exist, and the reasons why they would care, you've found the nub of what really makes what you do special: your Unique Value and the relationships that make it what it is. Once you've got this Unique Value in your sights, you must grab hold of it and keep it there. That value is the heart of the revolution.

At this point, it's worth pausing briefly to think in a little more depth about that elusive notion: *what customers want*. My exposure to business audiences all over the world has allowed me the rare, precious opportunity to be introduced to the nuances of customer demands at many levels, in many cultures. I speak to private and public sector audiences alike, at the very highest level of both commercial success and government influence, and as I've said before, we can substitute the word citizen for customer at almost any point in this book. As a speaker, what I try to do for my audiences is connect the dots on my personal radar screen, and depict the trends that are already under way, making real the possible impact on their businesses and individual careers.

In today's world of faster communication, longer working hours, unparalleled choice and seemingly infinite demands, one thing is crystal clear to me: everyone wants their life to be simplified. In almost every speech I've given, there is one particular interactive moment that perfectly demonstrates this point. I ask the audience, whether it's 100 or 1000 people, to raise their hand if they agree with the statement that follows. This statement is: 'I want my life to be more complicated'. Can I tell you, not one person, ever, in any audience, anywhere round the world, has ever raised their hand to say they agree. If you were to gather a roomful of your very best customers, and ask them the same question, I predict to you that not one would raise their hand. In this day and age, your mantra should be: *keep it simple.* Do not, ever again, in your entire career, introduce a customer service proposition that will complicate the life of even one single customer. Innovation is not about complexity, it is about giving your customers exactly what they want: a life less complicated.

If simplicity is at the top of the list of what customers want, right behind it is speed. Customers want your products or your services, not at the speed of *light,* but at the speed of *life,* their life, taking into account what they want as individuals. Think of it this way: if you are reading this book, you probably belong to a generation which can remember what it was like to use the very first computers. Casting your mind back, you probably remember what it was like to sit patiently while the disc, or even tape, which carried one basic

Who would come to your corporate funeral?

programme, took hours to load onto your machine. Fast forward a few years, you can probably remember your first internet connection. You would wait several minutes for the dial-up connection to load, and then several more minutes each time you wanted to navigate between pages. Today, in a broadband, Wi-Fi world, information zips around at the speed of light, we live in a time where everything online is instantaneous. Modern life is getting faster and faster and faster. Like you, your customers want products and services that give them what they want *now.*

The identification of Unique Value is your quest: pinpointing where it is, growing it, nurturing it, protecting it, sustaining it, helping everyone who works with you and for you to focus on it. Building the Common Purpose of your organisation around it, with service and products based on simplicity, speed, agility, transparency, honesty. Brand value based on under-promising and over-delivering. Brand value based on small kindnesses. Relationships which are not one-night-stands, which instead grow richer over time, where trust is built, earned and maintained, which provide Unique Value – Value for Life.

Let's take as an example a company which has created and sustained Unique Value through relationships perhaps better than any other in the current era: Apple. Right from the start, Apple has done something truly remarkable: it has made everyone who owned an Apple computer feel special and different, just that bit better. It's made them feel that they, wherever they are in the world, whoever they are, have a direct and powerful relationship with the company and the brand. Apple competes partly on products: it innovates enormously, takes risks and produces the most beautiful, desirable and user-friendly versions of key technological innovations. Apple never competes on price. It knows that it has established a place in the market where it sets the market price for each new product. Its competitors can take the lead from this, follow it or undercut it. The beauty of Apple is that it doesn't care. Apple's relationship with its customers allows it to operate in the market in this way. Beautiful, avant garde objects confer status and excitement on their owners. They also make life better, simpler and faster. People now trust Apple implicitly to do this. In 2008, *Fortune* magazine named Apple the most admired company in the United States, and in 2009 it became the most admired company in the world. Apple reputedly has the highest brand and re-purchase loyalty in the entire computing industry. This admiration, this customer devotion, is Apple's Unique Value.

Every year, at the Moscone Center in San Francisco, California, thousands of bloggers, journalists and tech geeks gather to hear Steve Jobs' latest announcement. With bated breath, these people hang on Jobs' every word; they are desperate to know what Apple has to say. Journalists all over the world eagerly hold front pages in anticipation of the launch of any new product, an event which is invariably shrouded in secrecy. Apple's product launches are meticulously planned: the product is in perfect working order, the stock is often already shipped to outlets across the world, and the sense of theatre is dramatic, especially when Jobs utters the magic words 'And just one more thing…', a moment which commentators have come to characterise fondly as the 'Steve-note'. People flock to these events partly because they feel that Apple's new products will guide the future of the tech world for many years to come. Yet it's more than that. They feel that by being there, by seeing Steve Jobs garbed in his black turtle neck and jeans, clutching the latest must-have product, they are establishing and reinvesting in their unique and special relationship with the company.

Of course, Apple's history as a company which creates Unique Value goes far back to the days of the launch of the Macintosh, and the infamous '1984' advert in the middle of the Superbowl, the yearly football extravaganza in America. Apple has always seen itself, and created its customer relationships, on the basis that it is groundbreaking and astonishing. Famously, Apple computers attract a different kind of user: educated, elite, creative. Apples have long been the chosen computers of designers and people who love not just what computers can do, but also how they look. Users of Apple computers are perfectionists; they want the best. As a company, Apple has been extraordinarily adept at creating and reinforcing this virtuous cycle of Unique Value through its customer relationships.

Everyone wants their life to be simplified

Most recently, however, Apple's flair for creating, building and maintaining Unique Value through relationships is perhaps best demonstrated by the launch and unparalleled success of Apple Stores across the world. Like the product launches, Apple Store openings are so highly anticipated that for the company's most dedicated users attending them can have the air of a pilgrimage. When New York City's Fifth Avenue 'Cube' Apple Store opened, the line stretched back half a mile. At Tokyo's Ginza store opening, thousands of people queued round eight blocks. This is the kind of customer relationship which almost every other business in the world could only dream of.

When Apple launched its stores, however, it was a much derided commercial decision. Retail was generally assumed to be in decline, the internet was booming and the heyday of the high street was thought to be a thing of the past. So what made Apple buck the trend? Quite simply, the fact that the entire store as an experience was constructed around the Unique Value which the Apple brand has to offer, and using the stores as a physical space to build relationships with the customer. Most computer stores are grey, dull places. They are places where most consumers take a deep breath, get what they came for and leave as soon as possible. Apple's stores are dramatically different. Bright, white and welcoming, they feel like a benevolent science fiction vision of the future. Every product is on display and can be touched and played with for hours on end. Perhaps Apple's greatest stroke of genius has been the 'Genius Bars' themselves. In each store, experts help users with technical problems. They do this without charge, and without overtly trying to sell anything in the process. It may seem counterintuitive to give so much away. Yet Apple has understood brilliantly that, by doing this, they establish and reinforce the relationship of trust, of friendship, of helpfulness, quite simply of Unique Value, which makes being an Apple user feel like something special and desirable, something which makes life better and simpler.

Apple's understanding of Value for Life goes far beyond just computer products. What made the iPod so extraordinarily successful was the fact that it gave customers exactly what they wanted before they even knew they wanted it. Of course, there were other MP3 players on the market, and many more being developed, before Apple launched the iPod. What made the iPod different, and so desirable, was that existing MP3s tended to be black, clunky-looking and off-putting to all but the most dedicated music fans and tech enthusiasts. Focus groups didn't necessarily say that people wanted the advantages of MP3s – all their music collection, portable and instant – in a beautiful, user-friendly package. What Apple did was to give people this before they even knew they wanted it. To boot, the iPod arrived on the market at a point in time when people were confused about how to access music online legally. By developing the iTunes store, Apple was able to capitalise on this. iTunes offered real 'Value for Life' by making the product easier to use, faster, simpler, and less complex. Not only could you carry all your music around with you for the first time ever. Not only did doing this make you look cool and design-conscious. Now, you could get any music, new or old, perfectly compatible for the iPod, in a matter of seconds. This is genuine 'Value for Life'. iPods, and later iPhones, are expensive items for most consumers. But that's never been the point. Their value isn't defined by their price, but by the value they offer, their beauty, their iconic packaging, and the coolness they convey on their users, and the relationship that Apple sustains through image and service. Apple understands implicitly that Unique Value is a moving target and that the value it creates through its one-to-one relationships takes much hard work to sustain. What it has done, and done very well indeed, is create and redefine Value for Life for an entire new generation.

Let's briefly return to the concept of Unique Value as defined by simplicity and speed. In the past decade, one company has uniquely altered our perceptions of both these aspects of consumer life, and that company is, of course, Google. Remarkably, you don't even pay for Google – not directly at least – but its value to users in almost every part of the world is so great because it gives them that most precious thing: any information they want, when they want it, in a simple format and with great speed. This is priceless.

A generation ago, it would have been unthinkable that you could have put down this book, typed a word or two into your computer, and then found out, in less than a second or two, exactly what you needed to know about almost any topic under the sun. Now try to imagine, however, what would happen if Google ceased to exist. Of course, there are other search engines out there, but you probably don't feel as strongly about them as you do about Google; they seem less trustworthy, simple, fast and reliable. If you're reading this book in Europe, there's a 90% chance that you use Google for almost all your online searches. Without Google, how would you do your job? How would you book your next holiday? How would you find out if there are any good restaurants in the area? How would your kids study and do their homework? The world without Google almost certainly seems like a much more confusing, less navigable place.

Google defines its Unique Value very simply as 'search'. This strong sense of definition is what allows Google to expand endlessly and with such great ease, whilst maintaining its billions of unique, one-to-one relationships with customers on every continent. Ironically, Google's genius insight came from understanding relationships better than any of its competitors. Not relationships with its customers (at this stage at least), but relationships between websites, using these as a more reliable way of ranking pages in a search than the existing model of just ranking pages according to the number of times a search term appeared on each page. That is a true Relationship Revolution. What the first group of Google users liked, and what drew others to it through word-of-mouth recommendation, was exactly its simplicity – whilst other search engine pages bombarded you with everything from the weather to celebrity gossip, Google was (and still can be) just a clean white page with a box on it, into which you can type your question, and wait a few milliseconds until another clean page appears, ranking your answers; speed and simplicity at their best. This is Unique Value. This is Value for Life.

As Google has expanded the range of services and products it offers, by keeping that simple idea of search at the heart of everything, it has been able to maintain and expand customer relationships. Google Earth has mapped out more or less the entire

Can you provide a clear, defiant and ambitious definition of the Unique Value of your business?

planet, but this is defined through searchability. Similarly, what makes Googlemail so appealing to its many users is its searchability and manageability. Google Page View aims to make the printed word as simple and searchable as it made the web. The reason for Google's success is that every single one of these things makes your life, as Google's customer, a little bit easier to organise. You may feel that the world is too complex, that there's too much choice and information. Google cuts out all that and usually takes you to exactly what you want to find. In an interview with the UK edition of *WIRED* magazine in 2009, Eric Schmidt, the company's CEO makes this very clear:

'The first question is, do you think search is a solved problem? And we do not. We think there are many, many things that can be done to improve search. Would you like to be able to say to Google "What should I do tomorrow?" or "Where are my car keys?" We're just at the beginning of answering the really hard questions…These are very, very hard problems, and search is the way to access these.'

This is an enviable understanding of the company's Unique Value, and the possibilities which this Unique Value provides for its customers.

Your searches, of course, don't provide Google directly with its income stream, 99% of which comes from advertising. And yet, for advertisers too, Google does exactly the same thing. With so many consumers out there and so much advertising spend wasted, Google lets advertisers target their products at people who've already said they're interested. At both ends of the value chain, then, Google has reached its unparalleled level of web dominance by providing the same kind of Unique Value.

Interestingly, both these companies, Apple and Google, have very similar origins, albeit several decades apart. Both companies were started by enthusiasts with limited resources. Steve Jobs at Apple, and Larry Page and Sergey Brin at Google, started out with limited resources, building their products as much if not more because they wanted to as for commercial gain. Because they wanted these products so badly, they understood why their customers would want them, they could see with great clarity where their Unique Value lay and took enormous leaps of faith to provide this. Of course, it's not just that simple. If Apple and Google hadn't been able to sustain such Unique Value over years, even decades; if they hadn't surrounded themselves with like-minded people who could see and believe in their Unique Value like they did, they would be light years away from the lauded companies they are now.

Could you provide as clear, as defiant, as ambitious a definition of your Unique Value as Eric Schmidt did in the above quote about Google? Do you and the people who work with you and for you really understand the Unique Value in your company in such fantastic, provocative terms? Do you really understand how to deliver on that Unique Value? How to protect it? How to nourish it? How to maintain it? Relationships are very fragile things. They are not a commodity. They are unique. To your business, they are uniquely valuable.

Today, more than ever before, failure to understand the Unique Value that you create through relationships is perilous in the extreme. In the post-recession era, customers are demanding value with every single transaction. Picasso once said, 'Bad artists copy, and great artists steal.' I openly invite you to steal ideas from this book and share them with all of your colleagues, to help focus your entire enterprise on building customer relationships to last a lifetime, together creating Unique Value – Value for Life.

Chapter 2

The Collapse of Trust and Confidence

On Friday 14 September 2007, queues started to form on the British high street. The evening before, the BBC's business editor, Robert Peston, had broken the news that Northern Rock, a high street bank known for high interest rates on savings accounts and generous mortgage deals, had sought a liquidity support facility from the Bank of England after experiencing problems in the credit markets. Ordinary savers started, with good cause, to believe that the Newcastle-based bank was in trouble. If the bank were to fail and go into administration, many worried that their savings might be wiped out.

So they queued. In the early morning of that Friday, people began to gather outside the branches in large numbers. As more people saw them, the queues themselves had a domino effect – if these people were so anxious, and you had money in Northern Rock, shouldn't you be doing something too? By the weekend, long orderly lines had started to snake round the bank's branches from Cardiff to Cambridge, from Glasgow to Golders Green. Branches remained open on the Sunday to cope with the level of demand. The people waiting patiently but anxiously to withdraw as much money as they could weren't used to taking to the streets in protest and fear. Many of them were over 50, conservatively dressed in fleeces and sensible shoes. Yet the level of anger in the queue was palpable. Often they had the best part of a lifetime's savings with the bank. It was only on Monday 17 that the queues began to dissipate, as the government extended the rate at which it would guarantee savings and took further steps to ensure the viability of the bank.

And yet these were people who had for years believed that a run on a bank was a near impossibility. The closest most people had come to seeing such a thing was in the film *Mary Poppins*, where Michael's reluctance to hand over his tuppence to Mr Dawes, his father's employer, sparked a similar crisis of customer confidence. In reality, Britain's banking system hadn't seen such panic in more than 150 years. Bank runs, people had been told again and again, were things of the past, quaint relics of a more precarious age, rendered impossible by the sophistication and reliability of the modern banking system. And, by and large, they trusted this advice.

Trust and confidence – the essence of commercial relationships – are largely intangible, so it's not often that you get to see what happens when they are absent. But what happened that weekend was a visual demonstration of the breakdown of these relationships and the impact that can have. The queues outside Northern Rock remain one of the most potent symbols of the human side of what turned into a global recession.

These people felt they had been personally betrayed. They were the people who had most trusted in the banking system. They had worked hard, saved hard, and played by the rules, to enable them to have thousands on deposit in a bank, for their retirement or for their children's or grandchildren's education. But Northern Rock hadn't fulfilled its side of the relationship, making risky investments in the US subprime mortgage market, relying to an absurd degree on wholesale funding, taking a cavalier attitude to the dangers involved, whilst key personnel profited to an unimaginable level.

Almost exactly a year later, when Lehman Brothers filed for Chapter 11 bankruptcy protection in 2008, it was the first global victim of the recession. The trust and confidence that ordinary customers and citizens had in their banking system bottomed out. People had been told, time and again, that a bank the size of Lehman Brothers was 'too big to fail', that such a thing simply could not happen. And then it did. The bank's aggressive expansion into precarious property-related investments led it to the point of no return. It made enormous write-downs. Across the world loyal employees lost their jobs. The dollar plummeted against the euro and the yen. While his bank had been losing millions of investors' money, Richard Fuld, the CEO, had been taking home millions in pay and benefits. At around the same time, Bank of America was forced to buy Merrill Lynch to stop it from suffering a similar fate.

The trust and confidence of ordinary citizens had bottomed-out

Northern Rock and Lehman Brothers have become emblematic of the credit crunch, and the financial crisis and recession that followed. This isn't another book about any of these phenomena. A great deal of ink has been spilled in trying to divine the root causes of the recession. A lot more is likely to be written on the subject for decades and even centuries to come, and it may be many years before we fully understand the complex web of over leverage, over confidence and the housing bubble that got us here. After all, *The Great Crash 1929,* J.K. Galbraith's masterful, canonical work on the twentieth century's greatest financial failure, wasn't written until 1954, 25 years after the event.

What I'm interested in here is what these events tell us about the collapse in consumer trust and confidence that we have experienced in recent years. What we must understand about these events is that the value lost through the financial crisis has been far more than the money wiped off shares on the Dow Jones or the FTSE 100. As I demonstrated in the previous chapter, real value resides not in these fluctuating indices but in the one-to-one relationships which organisations have with their customers. The queues outside Northern Rock and the cynicism in the wake of Lehman Brothers show that far greater value, with wider ramifications, has been lost in the recession.

Dick Fuld of Lehman Brothers, Adam Applegarth, the CEO of Northern Rock, and especially Fred Goodwin, the disgraced CEO of Royal Bank of Scotland, were all criticised for their arrogance. It seemed to those who watched their nonchalance in the days and months after their disgrace that they believed they had been invincible, that they had taken for granted the immense remuneration they had received, and believed that, whatever they did, however they ran their businesses, they had a right to do it that way. That is what stuck in the throats of their customers most. Ordinary people were incensed by this.

How dare the people who lost their money not suffer? How dare they have taken such risks in the first place?

Many customers had banked with the same company ever since they were children, and certainly all of their adult lives. Over the course of years, they built up a reliance on these institutions that goes far beyond the actual pounds and dollars they had on deposit there. They trusted what the bank's advertising reassuringly told them about the bank's prudence and excellence. They listened to, and followed, the bank manager's advice about the best savings accounts, mortgages and loans. As the financial system came crashing down, all these beliefs were called into question, and it seemed as if their faith had been badly abused.

Customers everywhere are very, very angry. The 2009 Edelman Trust Barometer survey shows that 62% of respondents spread across a sample of 20 countries reported that their trust in business was lower than it had been in the previous year. Just because you don't see them on the streets that often it doesn't mean you can afford to ignore how angry they are. For businesses, the way customers have chosen to respond to all this is far worse than overt anger. The cynicism that has come to dominate how individuals view organisations is extremely damaging.

Of course, even before trust and confidence came crashing down in this way, customers had become very cynical. What we are witnessing now is the acceleration of a trajectory of disappointment and frustration. What has caused this? I believe there are two factors involved here.

First, as marketing and advertising have become more and more sophisticated, promising the consumer a better life and better value, customers have come to believe this less and less. The growth of what Seth Godin calls the 'TV-industrial complex' has in some respects brought about the demise of the businesses it sought to promote. Sick of being treated as no more than the atoms making up a mass market, customers have reacted against this, believing less and less of what they see as the 'spin' and 'spiel' that emanates from businesses. A Nielsen survey of 2007 showed that, in the US, only 55% of consumers claimed to trust advertising. In the UK, the same figure drops to 48%, less than half the population. In Italy, it is as low as 32%, and in Denmark it is lowest in the world, at 28%. Such figures indicate that advertising and traditional marketing as ways of interacting with, and building up relationships with customers and consumers, are no longer effective. Social change has led to customers becoming far savvier and more confident in their own opinions. They are highly unlikely to trust an advertising slogan when their everyday interaction with an enterprise consists of indifferent service or poor quality goods. This is the 'Promise Gap' which I'll go on to discuss in far more detail in the next chapter.

Customers, everywhere, are very angry

In recognising this, many companies have stepped their marketing up a gear, to explicitly recognise and engage with this scepticism. Post-crisis, for instance, several banks have used adverts that play upon customers' perceptions of bad banks, offering poor service to high-street customers, implicitly trying to distance themselves from this and show that they are rooted in communities, prudent lending and sensible saving. Yet, in some ways, all this serves to do is to ramp up the level of cynicism one more notch – banks know that you're feeling cynical, they can even make jokes about it, but they can't, or won't actually do anything about it when people visit to pay in cheques or take out loans.

The second factor in the collapse of trust and confidence is the drip drip of negative press and revelations about companies that came out in the years prior to the recession. The Enron scandal is probably the most famous example of corporate malfeasance this century. Yet linked to this, and perhaps more indicative of the effects of lying to your customers, is what happened to the Arthur Andersen accounting firm as a result of its involvement in the Enron affair.

Based in Chicago, Arthur Andersen once joined PriceWaterhouseCooper, KPMG, Ernst & Young and Deloitte in the ranks of the 'big five' global accountants. For well over 100 years, the firm had been one of the most respected names in the business. Up until his death in 1947, Arthur Andersen himself, the firm's founder, had been one of the staunchest proponents of honesty and integrity in the profession. His personal motto had even been 'think straight, talk straight'. He firmly believed that accountants' main relationship of trust ought to be with investors, not with their clients' management. As with the banks, the thought that Arthur Andersen could go out of business was unthinkable. And yet it did, almost overnight. On 15 June 2002, the company was convicted of obstruction of justice. The jury found that employees had shredded files relating to its audit of Enron, thereby implicating it in the Enron scandal. The ramifications of this verdict caused the company to surrender its CPA license, the ultimate symbol of trust and confidence in its ability to practise honestly.

Three years later, in May 2005, the US Supreme Court unanimously reversed the verdict, finding fault with the way that the jury had been instructed. From a commercial point of view, however, that didn't make the slightest bit of difference. Andersen's reputation has been so badly undermined that its name on an audit is now highly undesirable. Though the partnership has not been formally dissolved or declared bankruptcy, over 85,000 jobs were lost. This is a prime example of what the collapse of trust and confidence means in practice. The power of Andersen's personal integrity was subsumed by images of shadowy corporate criminals shredding crucial documents. The relationships which had made Arthur Andersen strong, and had taken years to build up, were ruptured. These relationships were also complex and interconnected, since a successful accountancy practice needs to be trusted by clients, investors and ultimately by the SEC and the government. Without these relationships, the company is a broken shell.

It's also important to recognise that customers lead dual lives. They are not just consumers, they are also citizens. Much of what I've said in this chapter about the collapse of trust and confidence can be applied to the political sphere just as much as it can to the commercial world. Cynicism, anger and frustration in one area of public life breed more of the same in the other. Trust and confidence in politics and politicians is at an all-time low. Back in 2005, when the financial crisis was a distant nightmare, a survey carried out by the BBC suggested that 80% of UK voters did not trust politicians, and 87% did not believe politicians would deliver on their promises. The world of business seems almost healthy by comparison.

It is a similar deluge of misrepresentation, misinformation and a refusal to say 'I'm sorry' and mean it, which has created such mistrust. In the UK, the MPs' expenses scandal exposed a hidden culture which seemed petty and ultimately self-serving. Gordon Brown's famous promise as the British Chancellor of the Exchequer that there would be no return to boom and bust economics now feels decidedly hollow.

As a result, the population at large feels that in both areas of public life, as citizens and as consumers, very few organisations and institutions have been deserving of their trust. Without that trust, the relationships on which political and commercial life are based become null and void.

Both trust and confidence go far beyond politics and the collapse of financial markets. To return to our analogy of business relationships with personal relationships, these are healthy and productive when they are based on respect. When businesses no longer seem to respect their customers, taking them for granted, or even mocking their demand for the products they sell, the results can be nothing short of catastrophic. In this respect, the case of Gerald Ratner bears repeating as perhaps the ultimate example of such a breach of trust and confidence. Ratner was the owner of the successful jewellery chain, Ratners, which throughout the 1980s could be found in every British high street. During its ascent, the chain had shocked the staid British jewellery industry with its relentless focus on price and bold posters proclaiming just how cheap the merchandise was. Yet because it made seemingly 'luxury' goods available to a wide audience, the British public loved it. After Ratner gave a speech at the Institute of Directors in 1991, however, all that changed almost instantaneously. Explaining why he was able to sell products so cheaply he said he 'sold a pair of earrings for under a pound, which is cheaper than a prawn sandwich from Marks & Spencer, but probably wouldn't last as long'. The gaffes didn't end there either. He went on to explain that he was able to sell a cut-glass sherry decanter so cheaply because it was 'total crap'. Ratner later claimed that he made the remarks at a private function, and hadn't expected them to be reported in the media. Unfortunately for him, the British press and broadcasters pounced on the story, so much so that almost two decades later, this kind of blunder is referred to as 'doing a Ratner'. More than £500 million was wiped off the company's shares, and Ratner resigned a year later. The customers who had previously been pleased and proud to purchase these very same earrings and decanters, to wear them, serve drinks from them and give them to friends, suddenly deserted the company like rats from a sinking ship. They were angry, and felt they had been duped – nobody wants to give a present that's 'total crap'. And all this, because of the contempt shown for customers in an off-hand remark.

Let's dig a bit deeper, though, and consider in more detail what trust and confidence are based on, and how they interact to form the basis for a one-to-one relationship. First, it's important to define what we mean by trust and confidence in the context of business relationships. Trust is the *feeling* of faith in the actions and motives of another person, group or institution; to have a sense of your ability to rely on that person or body both now and in the future. Confidence is the way you behave as a result of that feeling of trust.

When businesses no longer seem to respect their customers, the results can be catastrophic

Both confidence and trust have long been recognised as key factors in the economy. They form part of the Keynesian notion of 'animal spirits': the non-rational, psychological factors that animate economic life. It's well known that financial crises are generally the product of a collapse of trust and confidence in the system, a belief that shares are overvalued in relation to the 'real' economy. In the recent crisis, it was growing concern about the quality of the subprime mortgages bundled together in CDOs which caused the edifice to crumble. The role of trust and confidence in customer relationships is less well known, but just as important. As we discussed in the previous chapter, the concept of value in business goes far beyond measurable notions of price and return on investment. Value lies just as much, if not more, in unique one-to-one relationships, and it is intimately linked to more quantifiable notions of wealth. When relationships are totally destroyed, as they were by Gerald Ratner, as they were by Northern Rock, and as they have been by an entire slew of politicians, it doesn't take long for the accounting to take note of this. What you didn't think you could measure suddenly becomes all too tangible, and you'll find that it's very often in millions and even hundreds of millions.

As I've said, when the trust and confidence in a relationship vanishes, it can be hard, almost impossible, ever to get it back. Yet it can be done. Rebuilding a relationship takes years of work, but it is possible. In the next chapter, I go on to look at this in more detail, to open up the notion of the 'Promise Gap' which is left when trust disappears, and to consider what you can do, as a business leader, manager or employee to bridge that divide.

Chapter 3

Closing the Promise Gap

Nothing threatens the longevity of a relationship more than broken promises. Except, of course, lies. Broken promises betray trust; lies multiply the damage and the rot. If you accept the basic premise of this book that customer relationships will be *the* dominant factor in determining success in the post-recession era, then you must become obsessed with closing the Promise Gap, which exists in every company, including yours. The Promise Gap is very simple and very lethal: it is the difference between what you say to a customer and what you actually deliver.

Our collective cynicism, about government and business alike, is made manifest by this gap. This recession has made our cynicism go 'nuclear', with a critical mass of explosive anger and rage at the incompetence and the lies as the global financial system approached meltdown. Customers are in no mood to give you the benefit of their doubt any longer. The oxygen of their rage is the broken promises they have come to expect. Their capacity to punish you now is unlimited, and their willingness to do so needs no encouragement.

You know exactly what these Promise Gaps are in your own life as a customer and as a citizen. You know how angry they make you, how often you discuss them with family, friends, colleagues and members on any online community to which you belong. Are you equally aware of where these gaps exist in your own organisation? Are you equally aware of how your own customers are reacting, who they are talking to and what is being said about you? Are you abundantly clear about the kind of damage these Promise Gaps are inflicting on the relationships you have worked so hard to build and maintain? Do you lie awake considering the amount of value draining away because customers are not only dumping you because of broken promises, they are also likely to denounce you, your company, your products, your staff, your ethics and your service to many, many other people?

I'd like to talk about a spectacular example of a broken promise that happened recently in an industry, and to a company, very close to my own heart. This was the opening of the new British Airways Terminal 5 at London's Heathrow Airport in early 2008. To put it bluntly, this was an event which left me speechless and, finally, heartbroken. The opening of Terminal 5 was perhaps as explosive an example of overpromising and underdelivering seen as any in the past several years. Although the events unfolded in the UK, the effect, and indeed the publicity, was truly global.

Customers are in no mood to give you the benefit of their doubt

The hype in the build-up was relentless. Day after day, the airline's senior executives appeared on TV, on radio and in print to sing the praises of the new terminal. On paper, it did sound extremely impressive. Designed by the Richard Rogers Partnership, it had been nineteen years in the making, following the longest planning enquiry in British history. The eventual cost of the project was more than £4 billion. Terminal 5 was to be used exclusively by BA, giving the airline a flagship hub on home soil. It would, according to the advance publicity, herald a new era in air travel. Gone would be the days of unmoving queues at the check-in desk, even longer queues to get through security, and endless hours in the limited and boring duty-free shopping and eating areas beyond that. Instead, this was a terminal built around the principles of online check-in and fast bag drop. It would feature less traumatic, less protracted security; and the choice of shops, champagne bars and gourmet restaurants, alongside the regular airport stores, would be almost limitless. Arriving at Terminal 5, your baggage would be far simpler and easier to reclaim, and you could be out and on your way as quickly as possible. On top of all that, it would be lighter, brighter and more human – filled with airy spaces and breathtaking views. Anticipating this opening, the thought of travelling through Terminal 5 did seem like one of the most exciting promises that the travel industry had to offer. BA's website described the vision for Terminal 5 as:

'A once in a lifetime opportunity for us to redefine air travel… to replace the crowds, queues and the stress with space, light and calm…to change the way you fly forever.'

This is pretty heady stuff. It sounded as if it would be travel Nirvana.

During all of this promising, I was literally shouting at the TV in frustration every time I heard about it. Why? As anyone who's worked in the airline industry could tell you, new airports and new terminals are almost invariably a nightmare in the early days; in particular the baggage delivery systems and its supporting software. In my years of involvement in and around the industry, I've seen disaster after disaster happen at similar openings in Denver, Bangkok, Hong Kong and many more. What made those involved in Terminal 5 think that this time it would be any different? Certainly, BA and BAA (the British Airports Authority) had invested a great deal in getting things right, but this was far from being any kind of guarantee of immunity from disaster.

Sadly, on the day that Terminal 5 opened for passenger use, 27 March 2008, it seemed that everything that could go wrong did go wrong. It swiftly became all too apparent that the new terminal was unable to cope with the volume of passengers who were travelling through. BA was forced to cancel scores of flights and close all flights to baggage check-in. Over the next ten days, nearly 500 flights were cancelled, and over 28,000 bags did not travel at the same time as their owners. A typical story was that of a passenger who had been flying to an Indian wedding in California, as part of a large family group. After waiting several hours to board, these passengers had been held in the plane, on the tarmac, for two more hours. Only mid-air were they told that their luggage might not actually be with them on the flight, leaving them desperate for the eight-hour flight at the prospect of arriving at a family wedding without presents or clothes. When they arrived in San Francisco – no luggage, no clothes, no wedding presents, no apology.

Story after story after story like this filled the airwaves, TV screens and newspapers. Back on the ground in London, angry, tired and frustrated customers began to pile up in the terminal's check-in concourse. All over the world, business meetings, conferences, family reunions and holidays were being compromised. The media jumped on these images, feeding a relentless stream of furious vox-pops, as news spread internationally of this corporate fiasco. The problems were blamed on a failure of the terminal's new IT system and also on insufficient staff training and systems testing; all of which seemed fairly basic to the man or woman in the street. How could you spend so much money without even making sure that the computers worked? Why did you promise so much? Why were you not prepared to better recover the situation? The damage was as deep as it was undeniable.

Today, travelling through Terminal 5 is a delight. Whilst you might not go so far as to claim that it has 'changed the way you fly forever' it does seem infinitely faster and more pleasant than many of Heathrow's older terminals, and most other terminals and airports around the world. If only there hadn't been such a gap between expectation and reality, between what was promised and what was actually delivered, this might have been the overriding public perception of Terminal 5.

Putting it right, however, has been a gargantuan task of service recovery. The debacle of the way that Terminal 5 opened became a PR nightmare, forcing BA to invest even more in an unplanned and very expensive advertising campaign which showed relaxed passengers smiling calmly in peaceful surroundings. Posters displayed around the UK boasted that they depicted the terminal as recently as that very morning, and featured statistics of the percentage of flights to arrive on time, or the time through check-in, under the heading 'Terminal 5 is working'. Only by inviting customers to sample something far more ordinary and witness for themselves what it was really like, could BA and BAA begin to dispel the negative press and public perceptions. Yet the damage done in those first few days, by over-promising and under-delivering, is likely to have negative consequences that will last for years in the minds of many.

How do you close the Promise Gap? With speed, simplicity and humility. I identify four clear stages in what I call the Profitable Art of Service Recovery. These are:

1.   Identify the problem
2.   Tell the truth
3.   Say sorry — and mean it!
4.   Fix it

What people are apt to remember and comment on are not the things that go perfectly first time, but the actions you take to make it right when something has gone wrong. In the age of online communities, denial and delay can threaten all of your customer relationships regardless of their longevity, and therefore bleed value from your company and seriously damage your profitability.

Let's turn to another example of the Promise Gap, this time in government, which seems to dwarf the Terminal 5 saga by comparison because the result was tragic and deadly. It is an example

Close the Promise Gap with speed, humility and simplicity

of how the feeling of being lied to can corrode relationships with citizens as well as with customers, and where the gap between what was promised and what actually happened loomed very wide indeed for much of the entire world to see.

I'm referring to the Iraq war, and the promises that were made to so many citizens in countries across the world about weapons of mass destruction and the need for war on that basis. This was the promise, the hype, the bargain which politicians made with their electorates, which is not really so very different from the bargains that companies make with their customers every day. In 2003, George W. Bush in America, followed by Tony Blair in the UK and the political leaders of other coalition countries, insisted that the need to attack Iraq was real and pressing. This was on the basis of supposed intelligence that Iraq was in possession of and developing more chemical, biological and nuclear weapons of mass destruction (WMD), which posed a real and imminent military threat to the West. The now infamous UK dossier in support of the war claimed that Saddam Hussein's regime would be able to deploy such weapons in as little as 45 minutes, with potentially devastating effects. To citizens around the world, such claims seemed utterly terrifying.

During the build-up to the war, as the governments of the USA, UK, Spain, Poland, Australia, Italy and Denmark made their cases, many people remained firmly opposed to the war for a whole host of reasons. Millions of these people took to the streets to protest in over 800 cities worldwide in the February of that year. Many more, however, took the claims made by their leaders at face value, and trusted in the pacts that were being made at that time – after all, why would rational politicians risk going to war, if there really was no credible evidence that their own countries were under threat? Indeed, this conjunction of terrorism and WMD would have been the only legal justification for going to war. The other reason, mooted only briefly at the time, of 'freeing the Iraqi people' qualified as 'regime change', which would have been illegal.

As the tanks rolled into Iraq in March 2003, to many citizens it still seemed that the bloodshed, danger and upheaval must be a necessary evil to protect their own countries from attack and root out a terrorist threat. As the months and years progressed, however, British and American troops were failing to find any evidence of the hoards of weapons which their leaders had claimed to know about before the war.

This reality was at first met with an embarrassed silence, but suddenly mushroomed to become a global outrage. The gap between what was promised and what was actually happening here was colossal. Soldiers' lives and billions of dollars had all been staked on an illusory claim that citizens should 'trust us'. In early 2005, US intelligence officials announced that they would no longer be searching for WMDs in Iraq. The Iraq Survey Group, which had been set up to lead the search, concluded that Saddam Hussein's stock of such weapons must have been destroyed entirely in 1991, following the previous Gulf War. At this news, thousands of citizens across the world erupted angrily in street protests. Millions more, however, didn't take to the streets. They simply accepted that such a Promise Gap was a fact of life: politicians lied to you, you couldn't trust them at all, there was little point in getting involved in politics, never mind being excited about it, because it would inevitably lead to disappointment and disillusionment.

And yet, at no time during the Iraq war, or its bloody and protracted aftermath, did the politicians who had initiated it make a substantial effort to close the Promise Gap that had opened up between them and their electorates. Thinking back to the four simple steps I mentioned in regard to Terminal 5's recovery , very few politicians have had the humility to follow this through, believing apologies make them look weak. They may secretly know the problem, but telling the truth and saying sorry seem to have been far more difficult.

Instead, like all the worst companies, they prefer to deny the problem exists. And so the cynicism, the resentment and the broken relationships drag on and on.

Of course, far better than closing a Promise Gap as wide as the one that opened up over WMD in Iraq or, on a smaller scale, Terminal 5, is to remain constantly vigilant about over-promising and under-delivering, understanding the massive detriment it does to your business in the age of instant communication. That's the revolution. Speed and simplicity and no delay: everyone in your company vigilantly looking to identify Promise Gaps and, where they exist, to fix them if they can, fully understanding the value of doing so. That's the exciting and infinitely challenging thing about closing the Promise Gap – it's never just a one-off process. The Promise Gap threatens every business in the world, every day. The organisations that are succeeding today, and which will succeed in the future, are the ones which flip the equation on its head: they focus on under-promising and over-delivering. They are the businesses whose entire operation is geared towards transparency, honesty, accountability, openness and, when necessary, service recovery. This is the only way to create Unique Value, and to maintain strong, vital relationships with your customers, in the post-recession era.

Focus now on under-promising and over-delivering

Creating Unique Value is also about understanding what a promise is and what it is not. What a promise is not, and should never be, is about a promise of perfection. Perfection doesn't exist. It has never existed. Even in manufacturing, the industry which might come closest, true perfection is not possible. It's worth striving for, but we've all learned to accept a degree of realism about perfection. Today, more and more of us, particularly in the developed world, work in the far messier arena of the service sector. Governed as it is by fragile human interactions, perfection in services is never possible. Most people know this. They don't expect perfection. What they want is respect, recognition, good value, and honesty. What they demand is that when mistakes are made, the companies concerned follow the four steps earlier mentioned, holding their hands up, admitting it, honestly saying 'I'm sorry', and giving genuine reassurances that they will solve the problem. Do not deny the problem and never lie to a customer – *never*. Mark Twain famously once remarked: 'Lying is complicated, because you always have to remember what you said.' Crucially, then, you must be increasingly aware that broken promises today are seen to be lies, and companies and governments alike have much work to do trying to rescue and repair relationships when people feel they are being lied to.

There are, of course, examples of companies who have created Unique Value and Value for Life by simply getting the basics right day after day after day. They have not promised the earth, they simply set out to put customers at the heart of everything they say and do, and then deliver it consistently.

Perhaps the company that does this kind of modest, realistic, deliverable, and constantly-maintained promise better than any other at the moment, in a very unsexy business, is the vast British-based supermarket chain Tesco. Now the third largest retailer in the world, it has yearly profits in excess of £3 billion. In recent years, Tesco has become a company of almost epic proportions in the UK, with its operations also spreading further and further into Europe, Asia and the US market. Several years ago, it was announced that nearly one in every seven pounds spent in the UK was spent in Tesco. The business includes everything from city centre Tesco Metros and neighbourhood Tesco Express stores where you can pick up a few bits and pieces for a quick dinner, to enormous out-of-town Tesco Extra hypermarkets, packed to the ceilings with everything from food to clothing to books to DVDs to petrol.

Yet, for such a retail giant, Tesco's promise to the customer is surprisingly modest and unassuming. In advertising and in-store promotions, Tesco simply announces that 'Every Little Helps'. I believe this to be the most subtle yet effective advertising promise in modern British history. On the surface of it, this isn't really much of a promise at all. If you're willing to delve a bit deeper, though, the seeming modesty disguises a highly effective strategy. It tells us that, despite being a massive global corporation, Tesco is actually on our side. It knows what it's like to be part of a busy family, where there's never enough time or money. But it doesn't want to patronise us either – after all, who doesn't want to spend a bit less on the groceries and get a bit more for their money? Despite the rocketing profits, Tesco is really working to help *you*, the customer! In reality, this is a big promise dressed up as a little one. 'Every Little Helps' – a life less complicated, not more.

So how does Tesco go about over-delivering on its promise? It compares its prices to those of its big competitors relentlessly, to ensure that its offerings are amongst the best to be found in the market for whatever you want to buy. As the economic squeeze hit its customers at the end of 2008, Tesco responded rapidly to these newly-straitened circumstances by stocking discount brand versions of many products in addition to its normal ranges. For many customers, this was the promise made real. For Tesco, it was a very savvy commercial move, allowing it to fend off competition from low-price rival stores by enabling its customers to save money while continuing to shop in the more familiar, more congenial settings of their local Tesco. Finally, Tesco benefits from having a Chief Executive, Terry Leahy, who has obsessively and overtly created a culture where customers are put at the heart of everything that is important to the business.

This promise has created much, much more in terms of value for Tesco than just allowing it to stay profitable in the teeth of a global recession. Customers feel that Tesco is a brand which stands by them, is on their side. The fact that, under one roof, it stocks almost everything that a modern, consumer lifestyle could demand genuinely does make your life less complex. In 2005, a British journalist conducted an experiment where she lived for a month by consuming only things that were bought in Tesco. At the end of the experiment, she concluded that 'the only terrifying thing is how easy it all was…I haven't had to do without anything', which as we've seen, is a proposition with which it's very hard to disagree.

In 2009, in the wake of global recession and an unprecedented lack of trust in the established banking system, Tesco announced that it was going to make a fairly sizeable move into the banking sector, rebranding its Tesco Personal Finance Division as Tesco Bank. What allowed it to do this? The enormous trust it had built up and sustained with its customer base over the course of many years, seeming to stand by them through the ups and the downs. Unlike the existing banks, people genuinely trusted Tesco to be open and honest with them. Just as they felt betrayed by the mathematical complexity of dealings in the financial market and the huge bonuses being paid out to the very bank chiefs who had bankrupted the economy, they felt that Tesco would be able to offer something genuinely better. 'Every Little Helps'; creating genuine Value for Life. A true Relationship Revolution.

Vigilance over the Promise Gap demands that you try to under-promise and over-deliver, constantly, and even obsessively. You, and all of your colleagues, need to know what your promises really mean, and what they stand for in the eyes of your customers. You have to be willing to accept full responsibility for these promises, to hold your hands up and say 'I'm sorry' (and really mean it!) when something goes wrong, then sort things out as fast as you can. You must also filter these promises right through every aspect of your business, your culture and your values, so they touch every single person in the company, ensuring that every single customer gets a sense of what these promises mean in every single interaction with your company day after day after day. A revolution in clarity and a revolution of purpose.

These are big challenges. They are exactly what so many of the companies (and governments) who have failed recently have neglected to do. You ignore the Promise Gap at your peril. But if you are willing, today, to rise to the challenge of closing the Promise Gap, doing so could be the foundation of your success for years to come. Join this revolution: its beauty is its clarity and its simplicity. Focus now on under-promising and over-delivering, and reap the benefits.

Chapter 4

Customers in Control, Forever

The single most profound reality of the so-called information age is the fact that customers are now in control forever. It is the basic premise of commerce in the 21st century. This fact will govern the business world for the rest of your life, and for at least the best part of the lives of your children. Those who understand this will survive and those who do not will end up as the victims of a cultural shift of which the recession is but a small part.

This is the true revolution, and it's your customers who have already gone to the barricades. They will be swift and brutal in their judgement, with increasing power beyond your imagination. Albert Einstein once said: 'Imagination is more important than knowledge'. Be a genius and pay attention. There is

This is the true revolution, and it's your customers who have already gone to the barricades

real danger in the enormous power that your customers now have, and the even bigger amounts they are about to amass in the coming decades. As with every danger, however, there is also real, exciting opportunity. More than anything, I want this chapter to help you understand and come to terms with the enormity of what this means, make sense of it in the context of building one-to-one customer relationships to last a lifetime, and take advantage of the opportunities being afforded you.

If you over-promise and under-deliver you'll swiftly find out this other basic truth: there is nowhere to hide any more.

Yesterday, today and tomorrow, your customers were very likely online talking about you, your company, your products, your staff, your ethics, your values, your politics, your promises – and all in real-time. Smart companies join these discussions. Less smart ones still ignore them, and go on as they always have done. There is nothing more anachronistic in contemporary commerce than to describe what you do as 'creating value *for* your customers'. There is real peril in this notion. What every business must do, now and in the future, for years and years to come, is to create value *with* its customers. The great economist, John Maynard Keynes, whose name has recently been invoked so often to explain and mitigate the current financial crisis, once said: 'The greatest difficulty in the world is not for people to accept new ideas, but to make them forget old ones'. What old ideas about your customers, and the effect they can have on you, are you harbouring? How might they be endangering your business? How quickly can you decide what ideas to let go of, what ideas to forget, and by what process? This is a humbling thought: all of your priorities are not important. They never are. Remember, it's not about size, it's about focus. Reduce your priorities to what matters today and tomorrow, not what mattered yesterday.

This is not another book about what caused the recession, nor is it another book about the societal and technological impact of a culture of mass collaboration and participation. There are many, many very good books already written, which deal with exactly these phenomena. What I'm interested in is the revolutionary impact these have on the way that customer relationships are built and maintained, and the seismic effect they are having on commerce itself. The reality you must face is that customers *want* to be involved. The passive customer is an endangered species, likely to die out

The passive customer is an endangered species

within a generation. The new, active customer is infinitely demanding. When you annoy them, when you sell them short, when you over-promise and under-deliver, your customers now have the power to let everyone know about it hours, if not minutes, after it happens. You must believe this is true, and you must drive this notion to the point of acceptance in everyone around you.

Once a promise is broken, it stays broken, out there in the ether, contaminating the way other existing and potential customers see your business and your brand. This is like a virus; in fact, it's what I call 'emotional contagion'. Customer cynicism and anger is spread by such emotional contagion and, like swine flu or SARS, it will spread out of your offices, out of your call centres, out of your stores and out of your factories like wild fire. Cynicism, anger and mistrust can sweep the internet and the world in real-time, with devastating effects. The only difference between the emotional contagion of customer cynicism and the physical viruses that seem to threaten us is that, from a commercial point of view, cynicism is almost certainly more imminently lethal.

In the previous chapter, we talked about the necessity of closing the Promise Gap, and how failing to do so can leave your customers feeling angry, frustrated and cynical. Now, I want to talk about how this happens, and the commercial consequences that it's going to have for you.

Try this experiment to see what I mean. Search on Twitter for your company's name, or the name of another well-known brand. It's quite probable that hours, minutes, even seconds ago, someone was saying something about it. On their mobiles, from their Black-Berrys and from their laptops, people are commenting to their networks of friends and followers about the service they have just received, and the interactions they have just had. If it was great, they may well say so. If it wasn't, they almost certainly will. Now do the same kind of search on Google. As well as the official company website, and the journalistic articles you already know about, you'll probably find countless other mentions of the brand name on blogs and message boards. Google is a miracle, and it's free. You can do the same kind of thing on YouTube. These are unauthorised, unguarded, and unbelievably powerful.

Customer cynicism and anger is spread by emotional contagion

New films, for instance, can now suffer from what's been called 'the Twitter effect'. Previously, a much-hyped new film which wasn't actually up to much could still do quite well at the box office for a couple of weeks. Word that it didn't live up to its own launch, or the five star reviews on the advertising billboards, would filter out slowly, naturally limited by the number of people any one cinemagoer could or would tell about the experience. Not so any more. Today, dissatisfied moviegoers coming out the cinema can tweet their dissatisfaction to thousands, even millions of followers. Box-office takings for this kind of film now drop off noticeably in days rather than weeks. This isn't merely an interesting cultural observation. It's a fact of life whose veracity can often be counted in the millions of pounds or dollars to be made or lost.

Perhaps the best single example of this phenomenon of customer power is the story of Dave Carroll of the band Sons of Maxwell. Along with his band, Carroll was on a United Airlines flight out of Chicago to Nebraska, when a passenger behind him remarked that the baggage handlers seemed to be throwing guitars on the tarmac. Worried about his expensive Taylor guitar which he had checked as hold baggage, Carroll alerted several air stewards to this fact, but was met with complete indifference. Sure enough, when the guitar was lifted off the carousel in Nebraska, it was badly broken and beaten up. Angry and frustrated, Carroll complained to United Airlines, asking them to reimburse the cost of repairing the guitar. His pleas fell on deaf ears. Again and again, he was met with blank refusals to admit negligence or to compensate him for the repairs. Finally, after a year of dispute, he was given a definitive 'no' – there was absolutely nothing the airline would or could do. Frustrated and angry, Carroll channelled his protest in a different way. He recorded the song 'United Breaks Guitars', filmed an accompanying video – complete with background mariachis, indifferent air hostesses and lines taped to the ground representing the spot where the guitar met its end – and posted it on YouTube. The response was astounding. The lines:

> 'United, United, United, you broke my Taylor guitar;
> I should have flown with someone else or even gone by car'[1]

echoed around the internet.

At the time of writing, the video has had well over six million views on the website. It has had many thousands of ratings and comments, mostly furthering the bad feeling surrounding United, and providing a focal point for other gripes about the company and indifferent airlines in general. Carroll and his song have been featured on TV, radio and in the press around the world. United have contacted him personally to ask him to take the video down, but he has steadfastly refused, instead recording and uploading two more songs. In the media, United's response to the event has seemed

---

1 Carroll, D. (July 2009) 'United Breaks Guitars' (MP3 single), Sons of Maxwell, http://www.youtube.com/watch?v=5YGc4zOqozo

distinctly lacking in surefootedness. It's a story that's hard not to respond to – the lumbering unresponsive corporation, brought to book by a little guy with (or without!) a guitar. If ever you needed proof that all this matters commercially, that it is far more than 'just' bad PR, think about this: as a result of the negative press surrounding 'United Breaks Guitars' United Airlines' share price plummeted by 10%, costing shareholders an estimated $180 million.

This is what your customers can do to you, indeed will do to you, if you fail to listen to them or engage with them. If you don't want to talk to your customers, there's every chance that they'll want to do the talking for you, and now they've got an unlimited audience. How will you prevent yourself from ending up in United's shoes? Do you know that you could react better than United if you did?

I believe that what Carroll did is just the start of something much bigger. Carroll created a customer community of people who were specifically frustrated with United, or who had just grown sick of the way that big airlines seemed to take their customers for granted. These customer communities, I believe, are the seeds of what will develop into Customer Unions. Such Customer Unions have the potential to be a thousand times more powerful than the Trade Unions ever were. Unlike Trade Unions, they're not fixed and the membership isn't limited. Anyone can join a Customer Union, and their numbers and mission are flexible, changing and developing to meet the needs and complaints of the moment.

Customer Unions will be composed of like-minded people, banded together, who will vote with their feet and their wallets when they see something, or are treated in a way, that they don't like. Consider what happened to Dell, for instance, when customers began to complain about their laptops catching fire in 2006. Customer discussions about the defective laptops had been circulating on the internet for some time when eventually someone posted a video of a laptop exploding at a conference in Japan. Millions of people saw it online, eventually prompting Dell to carry out the largest product recall ever seen in the consumer electronics industry, and make an embarrassing, shamefaced apology.

There are thousands more stories like this, of Customer Unions taking control, of forcing embarrassing climb-downs and costing corporations millions. These stories exist in every industry, in every part of the world. You almost certainly know your own. The scary thing about Customer Unions is that, unlike Trade Unions, you can't just shut them out and keep a 'closed shop'. Customer Unions, by their very nature, will be composed of your customers. How long do you think you'll survive when they're shut out completely? You can refuse to negotiate with a Trade Union any time, but announcing that you're not prepared to talk to your customers in this day and age is an absurd response. Trade Unions were reassuring because you could see them; you knew who was on the picket lines and why they were there. Their demands, blazoned on placards, were easy to make sense of. Customer

Unions, by contrast, are amorphous; they're hard to actually pinpoint. But that makes knowing they're there, and talking to them all the time, a thousand times more important. By working together, your customers can either reward you lavishly when you get it right or, more likely, punish you brutally when you get something wrong.

Once you've accepted just how real and harsh this all is, it's important to think about *how* you are going to collaborate with your customers, how you are going to let them participate, and create their Value for Life, with you. Take this example. If you look back at the last ten years, you'll see that reality TV shows and serious broadsheet newspapers have experienced almost entirely different trajectories. You may not like this, I don't particularly like it either, but it's true. Reality TV shows have presented people with the forum they want, indeed need, to participate in the creation of the content they consume. From *American Idol* to *Big Brother*, consumers get most engaged and find most reward when they believe that the fate of the programme is in their

Customer Unions have the potential to be a thousand times more powerful than Trade Unions ever were

hands. They reward the people they like and punish those they don't. They are fickle and passionate at the same time. At its height, more than five million people, or 10% of the UK population, were tuning into *Big Brother*. In an age of multi-channel media and audience fragmentation, that's hard to argue with. By taking advantage of these trends, companies like Endemol, the creators of *Big Brother*, have made millions. *Big Brother* may have had its day. Be assured, though, that the phenomenon which replaces it will only have understood these trends better, and be able to give consumers a more exciting way to participate.

Newspapers, in stark contrast, seem to be experiencing their death throes. Used to a passive audience which wanted no more than to be handed what the *New York Times* calls 'all the news that's fit to print' from on high, almost no serious newspaper has managed to adapt to a world in which consumers want to create, collaborate and participate rather than just consume. The addition of message boards and forums for comment at the end of a newspaper article is in reality no more than a plaster over a far greater, gaping wound. Giving the content away for free online has led circulation to haemorrhage with few corresponding editorial benefits. Newspapers which once seemed inextricably part of the landscape of their respective cities are being forced to shut down at an unprecedented rate, and their plight is now well documented. In a world where consumers want to collaborate, contribute and participate all the time, the problem for serious newspapers seems to be that they just didn't get it fast enough. As Keynes would have said, they hung on to their old ideas for far too long. Your customers now have four things that have forever changed the balance of power in all commercial relationships: *information*, *choice*, *power* and *control*.

Through collaboration and participation, they will use each of these things to create their own forms of Unique Value. You cannot give these things away because your customers already have them. You need to accept this reality, deal with it, and plan to somehow take advantage of it.

Information

You need to publish and share every legal piece of information about who you are and what you do. If not, a competitor will to your distinct disadvantage. How else can your customers know enough about you to help you create value? Your customers are in control, and people in control tend to want all the information they require to make a decision. A great example of sharing company information in a brave, new, extremely creative and indeed very profitable way has been documented by the great chronicler and theorist of collaboration, Don Tapscott in his book *Wikinomics*. Here he describes just how sharing such information, and allowing such collaboration, created enormous wins for the mining company Gold Corp. Several years ago, the company was failing to turn up enough finds. It seemed that nothing worked, and its fortunes − and its share price − had entered what seemed like terminal decline. That is, until it discovered a radical solution. It published all of its most sensitive data − its maps, its geological surveys, everything − and offered a reward to anyone who could help it successfully prospect for gold. That might have seemed like commercial suicide. Anyone could access this information, including the company's competitors. And yet, helped on by collective wisdom from those outside the company, including its customers, Gold Corp was able to substantially increase its finds, and therefore its share price. Gold Corp turned information into participation, collaboration and, eventually, tangible commercial success. In the process it built invaluable relationships right across the communities that it served. Mining seems like a pretty old-school industry. That's one of the things that's so interesting about this story. Whatever industry you're in, however much you might think collaboration is difficult for you to do, how are you doing this for the communities you relate to?

Choice

Choice gives people freedom, the freedom to be very promiscuous and leave you tomorrow for one of your competitors. The amount of information available today makes this freedom turbo-charged. Nothing makes the preciousness and value of individual one-to-one customer relationships more clear than the acceptance of this reality. Everyone who works with you and for you should be obsessed with this reality. What people think and say about you matters more than ever before. Word of mouth and reputation are more important than advertising. You have to be obsessed with that reality. Consider how a user-generated review gives customers everywhere an unparalleled level of information provided by someone who has actually experienced your product or service, and how much more powerful this is than the advertising spend you are trying to justify. These reviews have changed how choices are made in many industries and for many products. Think about travel. When you book a hotel, how often do you check out the reviews on TripAdvisor? When you book a restaurant in a new city, do you check it out on TopTable or a Zagat guide? You might well take what these sites say with a pinch of salt, but you almost certainly have a look at them – and when was the last time you booked a hotel or restaurant that had universally negative reviews by people who had already been there? Or, how reassuring do you find it when your choice is confirmed by dozens of voices who tell you just how good it was? With so much choice giving people so much freedom you need to realise, now, just how many alternatives there are for customers who don't like you and what you do, and just how easy it is for them to find out about what these alternatives are. In a world of unmitigated choice, relationships are the only things that will keep your customers coming back for more.

Power

Customer Unions will wield tremendous power in the near future, even more than they do today. But how can you, as a business leader in these revolutionary times, give at least some of this power to your consumers before they seize it from you? Since we're talking about power, perhaps an example from politics is most germane here – the word 'citizen' can be substituted for the word 'customer' almost anywhere throughout this text.

One of the most talked about, groundbreaking aspects of Barack Obama's victory in the 2008 US presidential election is the way he seemed to devolve as much power as possible to his grassroots supporters. By giving this power to them, he got even more back in return. By allowing his supporters to collaborate and participate, he strengthened their relationship with him, creating ultimate value for him and for themselves. In the state of Ohio, for instance, Democratic campaigners gave farmers the template to paint the Obama campaign logo on their barns. They did it themselves, but it was an empowering piece of campaigning, and this genuine devolution of power to the grassroots created a strong relationship between Obama and the rural Ohio citizens who supported him, so vital to his victory in a keenly contested state.

Similarly, the Obama campaign created a social networking site, myBarackObama.com, allowing supporters to interact not just with the campaign, but with each other, right across the country. It is said the campaign sent out emails to nearly 13 million people every day! This gave the recipients of these messages an enormous amount of power, yet in turn it created an enormous amount of value for the campaign because people felt included, informed and therefore empowered. This bold new way of campaigning spelt an end to the way that political campaigns had been conducted in the US and across the world forever. Gone are the days where political campaigns centre around a shiny campaign bus and a slickly, controlled, top-down PR machine ready to spin its candidate's message for that day's news. From now on, if candidates are unwilling to give a bit of power to their supporters, the reality is that they're unlikely to get much back.

If you're a business leader, and this seems to be very far away from the way that you interact with the people who consume your products or use your services, you ought to be very afraid by now. After all, Obama is a politician, and politicians have always been famous for adopting ideas like this many years after they are part of the business lexicon or the mindset of the population at large. When New Labour won the UK general election in 1997, partly through mastering the dark arts of political 'spin', all they had done was grasp the kind of PR that most businesses had been proficient at for several years. If political campaigns are harnessing the power of giving power away, why aren't you? If such tactics can help Obama to come from nowhere to win an election, what could it do for your business? Remember that your future customers, your future citizens and your future employees are not yet spending money so you're probably not tracking what they want and what they value. This is, however, a generation that has grown up with the internet as a fact of life, that takes all this choice and power for granted.

Control

This is closely related to power, but it's far from being the same thing. Your customers are now in control forever. You have a choice: you can either let them feel that control, let them take advantage of it, or you can watch them walk away from you to someone else who does just that. Unless you have a monopoly in your industry, your relationship with your customers is naturally asymmetrical: they can walk away from you, but you can't walk away from them nearly as easily. You may think that you have more money and more resources than any single one of them, and that's very likely true. When your customers get together, though, when they understand what control they have, the true balance of power becomes very clear.

I'd like to use another political example here to demonstrate just how truly revolutionary both customer control and citizen control have become in the information age. Think back to the Spanish election of 2004. Throughout the campaign, it had looked as if the election would be won fairly easily by the Partido Popular, the incumbent party then in control of the government. When a series of bombs went off on commuter trains on their way into Madrid on 11 March (three days before the scheduled general election), the government was quick to denounce the attack as the work of ETA, the country's Basque separatist group. But the Spanish people were suspicious and cynical. Much of the emerging evidence linked the attack to Islamic terrorists. The government's determined and blinkered attempts to discount this evidence and continue to pin the blame on ETA rang hollow with the electorate, which feared that the attacks had been carried out by Islamists in revenge for Spain's PP-led involvement in and support of the Iraq war. Within a matter of three days, the historical course of the country was changed forever. Spanish citizens, using the power and freedom of their mobile phones, seized control. Demonstrations were swiftly organised across the country, demanding news from the investigation. Such discontent mobilised a group of voters who had not planned to vote, and had perhaps never voted in the past. They took control, and went to the ballot boxes deliberately to punish the PP for what they believed was its deception. On 14 March, the opposition PSOE came to power. This is the power of citizens today when they know they're in control. If citizens are now seizing control pay attention! So are your customers.

The companies that will be successful in the future are the ones who are not intimidated by the power of customers, who are willing to continually work with this power to create better products and better services for their own commercial advantage. In the UK, for instance, Carphone Warehouse has started to publish customer complaints on its website to publicise its commitment to corporate transparency and accountability. Globally, the company Bazaarvoice has created an entire industry out of providing the technology to host customer reviews.[2] Samsung Electronics, which uses Bazaarvoice's services, has reported that such responsive-

2 *The Financial Times*, Thursday 3 September, 2009

ness to customers has had an enormous impact on the way that the entire company works. For example, after customer feedback indicated that the first model was too wide to fit in most conventional TV cabinets, the company was forced to change where speakers were placed on their large, flat-screen TVs. The speed of the review process allowed the company to respond quickly, thereby rescuing it from being left behind in the marketplace. These companies, engaged in talking to and responding to their customers, are the smart ones.

The revolutionary battle with your customers in the future is likely to be a battle for their *attention,* as much if not more than a battle for their *spend.* No matter where in the world you're reading this, if you live in a big city, or even if you've visited a big city recently, you'll know what I mean. As you ride up the escalator from your subway station, LCD TV screens allow adverts to follow you all the way. As you stand in a station or airport concourse, far larger screens beam adverts, news and gossip down at you. Almost everyone now has the internet, even TV, on their mobile phones. In a matter of months, or years at the very most, screens will allow video inserts to become part of magazine adverts and flyers. I call this trend Daily Cinema Living. To our grandparents, the idea of moving pictures in the television at home may have seemed revolutionary, but now the moving image surrounds every one of us, blurring the boundaries between the lived reality and projected reality. Cinema used to be an enormous fixed screen, showing carefully developed Hollywood blockbusters to enraptured audiences. Now cinema is part of the fabric of our everyday lives; it's something that we observe, make and participate in for a large part of almost every day. Attention spans are getting shorter and shorter, and you need to be bolder and bolder to grab and hold them. This is at the heart of the creation of unique customer relationships.

That is the challenge that you, as a business leader, now face. It's what you must deal with as soon as you finish reading this book. How will you respond to the power of Customer Unions? How do you know what people are saying about you, and the impact that is having? How are you giving your customers, the people on whom you rely every single day, more information, choice, power and control? How are you grabbing and keeping their decreasing attention spans? It might be comfortable and reassuring to think that YouTube, Facebook, Twitter etc., are really just for kids. Get with it and get over it! These 'kids' are your future customers and the future has already arrived. How you devolve power to them and help them to create value with you will determine your long-term ability to succeed. Get ready for tomorrow by accepting that the revolution has arrived already.

Chapter 5

Get Closer, Get Smarter, Get Ready

Your biggest competitor is your own view of the future. What will the post-recession era look like? Who will your customers be? How will you communicate with them? How will they communicate with you? How will they communicate about you? Who will your customers trust? What will they value? What will value look like? How will you prepare your staff for these eventualities? How will you prepare your company? How will you prepare yourself?

Charles Darwin famously once said:

'It is not the strongest of the species that survives, or the most intelligent. It is the one that is the most adaptable to change.'

What Darwin said about nature in the nineteenth century has great resonance in the post-recession era, and it is directly relevant to you, your colleagues, your company and, indeed, your customers. Linked to Darwin's thinking, I have come to believe that intelligence is no longer a competitive advantage in the running of a business. That may seem like a radical proposition to you. If it does, just think about all the remarkably intelligent people who managed to bring the world economy to the brink of catastrophe. Think of all of the highly intelligent people you know personally who have not been able to adapt to new and challenging circumstances in their lives. When hiring today, perhaps you should try and ascertain not how clever someone is, but how adaptable they are. These are the kind of adaptations your business has to make to be relevant in the early twenty-first century.

Your ability to build and maintain customer relationships, create Unique Value and therefore Value for Life in the post-recession era, will be linked to your ability to understand, adapt and then respond to customer demands. Not their demands from five years ago or two years ago – the world now moves so fast that these are almost certainly no longer relevant – but what they want right now which will have changed as a result of the recession. You cannot guess. You have to know. The only way to do this successfully will be to set as a primary goal of your enterprise to get *closer* to customers than you ever thought possible. Your Relationship Revolution will be based on how ruthless you are in achieving this goal.

Getting closer will then allow you to get *smarter* in what you are trying to deliver and to get *ready* for success in the post-recession era. None of this requires complex business models to understand. In fact, very little in business does. In my own time in industry, I never hired a consultant who presented me with a matrix or management model. Anyone can use these to get mediocre results. Instead, I always told consultants that I wanted fresh, common-sense ideas. Part of the simplicity of this book and its message is the amount of common sense employed.

This recession has changed what people value. This one sentence alone should prompt you and your colleagues to consider necessary strategic and structural changes in how you operate your business. Are you close enough to your customers to understand what this means? What can you do to get closer? This recession has made people feel cynical, fearful, angry, doubtful, anxious and resentful. Every politician in the world is under pressure as a result. You are under pressure as a result. Are you close enough to your customers to understand how their resultant behaviour will affect your business? It's your responsibility to get as close as you legally can to your customers to find out exactly what they want. Only this will allow you to get smarter in delivering customers' every demand. In turn, this is the best way to get ready to succeed in the post-recession era. To quote Seneca, the famous Roman philosopher: 'Luck is what happens when preparation meets opportunity'.

Prepare now, make the changes necessary to redirect your focus towards building and maintaining customer relationships by getting these things right, by knowing – not by guessing. *Your biggest competitor is your own view of the future* Only this will allow you to create the Unique Value which means Value for Life for you and your customers.

How close is close enough? Take a walk down your local high street or main street. Pay attention to the examples that you see. The newsagent serving local customers knows what newspapers and magazines they want and does not need CRM software to advise him. The butcher knows the people who come into his shop, knows the cut of meat they require for their special dinner and will always have it on time for them. The dry cleaner knows exactly what day your clothes need to be ready for pick-up. Perhaps it's your financial advisor; that close. Perhaps it's your doctor; that close. In a world where businesses for many people seem too big, too global, too impersonal, and too out of control, these small examples of commercial closeness are often overlooked, but I believe they are the lifeblood of every economy in the world and perhaps the best examples in your own life of what close means. How could you learn from them, and be more like them in knowing your customers and their needs and their demands? It's unlikely that you'll be able to replicate exactly what they do, but you can be inspired by the spirit of what they do.

To see the risk involved in not being close enough to your customers, you need look no further than the most despised and most mocked invention of the information age, the call centre. When I'm speaking about customer service to large audiences anywhere in the world, there is always a predictable interactive moment that I employ. That is the moment when I ask everyone in the audience: 'Please raise your hand if the first thing you want to do when you go home today is to call a call centre'. In all the years that I have been doing presentations, not one single person has ever raised their hand in any audience anywhere in the world. Of course not! Call centres are perhaps the ultimate example of how using technology can create distance and frustration, rather than closeness and satisfaction, between companies and their customers. With every technological advance, call centres seem to get worse rather than better. How could we have got it so wrong? Everyone loathes being asked to press a series of buttons interminably. Everyone loathes the ridiculousness of voice automation. Everyone loathes the repetitive scripts that call centre workers are forced to parrot when confronted by a problem or anomaly. Faced with this kind of frustration, almost everyone voices the refrain that 'I just want to talk to a real person'. People want simplicity and speed, and service at the speed of life – their life.

Almost everyone you know will have a story about their worst ever experience with a call centre, be it the voice automation which went into a tailspin when faced with a regional accent, or the person on the other side of the world who had no understanding of the logistics of the railway journey you were booking. You may well have slammed down the phone yourself in fury at this mechanisation of the customer relationship. Pay attention! It is exactly what your customers are feeling when facing any analogous situation in their interactions with your company. It's a sad indictment of how wrong things have gone that many companies now make a virtue of the fact that they only use domestically-based call centres. The problem here, however, is not outsourcing, it is automation and what it does to the relationship and therefore to lifetime value. Moreover, everything that the companies who use call centres could be learning about their customers, their needs, their demands and their values, is being lost, disregarded for the most part by employees who know very little about the actual workings of the company they are supposed to service. If your company uses call centres, what's it costing in terms of lost information? Can you put a price on all the knowledge and understanding that is draining away through the world's phone lines?

This recession has changed what people value

Getting close to your customers is not about a one-night stand. It must be about a relationship that has the potential to last a lifetime. *That* close. Close enough to understand better than your competitors what people want, and why, and how to deliver it.

Smarter is at the heart of being able to turn closeness into tangible economic results for your company. Don't guess what your customers want. Know what they want. Please don't think that I'm talking about focus groups here. I'm not. By and large, focus groups are an old-fashioned, highly-flawed way of gathering information about your customers and insights into how they value you. Focus groups often outsource this collecting of information and too frequently absolve the people within an organisation from any responsibility for acting on it, never mind gathering it themselves in everyday interactions. In fact, focus groups often bring about distance where they should create closeness. Anyone can collect information. That does not make you smart. What makes you smart is how you adapt to the knowledge you obtain.

This is what being a 'Learning Organisation' should really be about. It is not about training, it is about having a business that is obsessed with learning from customers every day and adapting their products, services, values and culture to what they learn. Genuine learning organisations share their knowledge freely, respond to this information openly, and filter this understanding readily through everything they do.

Just as the passive customer is a dying breed, so too is the passive employee. Smartness and learning means knowing how to share this intellectual 'customer capital', giving it away to get more in return, connecting up the needs of your customers with concrete steps you can take to meet them. This book is all about value, and your ability to create value will be driven by your ability to construct viable platforms for your customers and employees alike to participate in idea generation that builds and maintains relationships. This is the action part of understanding that customers are in control forever. Collaboration must happen across borders, disciplines, companies and hierarchies. Business leaders today are facing a perfect storm of symmetrical needs – your customers and your employees are demanding new and dynamic platforms for communication, collaboration and participation.

For me, the perfect example of such closeness, smartness and collaboration is the business model devised by eBay over the past 15 years as it has acted as the world's online auction house.

Legend has it that the first item ever sold on eBay was a broken laser pointer. Pierre Omidyar, the company's founder, contacted the purchaser in astonishment, to ask if he knew that it was broken. The response came back 'I'm a collector of broken laser pointers'. By getting this close to customers, you're able to unleash demand that you could never otherwise have known existed. Today, with operations everywhere from Argentina to Vietnam, the company's simple business model of the auction has been able to replicate this closeness again and again. Yet this closeness could all be pretty meaningless if the company weren't smart enough to use it to create more demand. The eBay pulse site, for instance, provides real-time information on what is hot on the site, what terms are being searched for and what the largest online stores are. At various times, the company has also used discussion boards, blogs, wikis and chat rooms to increase the smart collaboration that exists between it and its customers, both buyers and sellers. eBay's relationship to its customers is that of the benign parents towards its children – happy for the most part to sit back and watch what they're doing with some satisfaction, ready to learn from them but willing to step in at signs of illegality or trouble. Though economic difficulties have given the company a rough ride, eBay remains proof that closeness and smartness really do pay off.

You are likely to have spent the last several months deciding what cuts to make as a result of falling sales, tight cash flow and a squeeze on resources. You may have spent long hours in the office, and lain awake at night wondering if you're making the right choices about what to cut, where to cut, how deeply and for how long. What has been your objective beyond the bottom line? What will be the long-term consequences of what you have done? Will it position you better to survive in the post-recession era? Did it target the fundamental issue of cutting bureaucracy? If not, why not? Without brutally cutting back your bureaucracy, getting closer and getting smarter are likely to remain no more than pipe dreams.

You have wasted this crisis utterly if you have not brutally and ruthlessly attempted to identify, root out, attack and kill bureaucracy wherever it exists in your organisation. I mean it, kill it. The terrible thing about bureaucracy is that it never helps a relationship be more successful. Wherever bureaucracy exists, it puts up a barrier between an organisation and the world outside it, and indeed barriers between people and purposes even within that organisation. People hate bureaucracy and they think it is evil, in business and in government. When was the last time you heard anyone say they

Call Centres are perhaps the ultimate example of how technology can create distance and frustration… between customers and companies

wanted more of it? The word that most often accompanies bureaucracy is 'nightmare'. It makes life more complex when people want simplicity. It makes things slower when people want speed. It wastes money and time when you need ef-ficiency more than ever. It makes you less close, less smart and less ready.

In the future, I believe, people will come to understand this recession as, partially at least, a crisis of bureaucracy. Layers of bureaucracy prevented people from understanding how near the entire financial system was to the precipice. So distant were the chiefs of the large financial institutions, so many layers were there between them and the traders and analysts who were making the decisions, so far were they from the risks in the market, that the crisis came to them as an unwarranted surprise. A 2009 study by the Advanced Institute of Management Research[1] confirmed this view, arguing that these layers of bureaucracy allowed many executives within the banks to take on huge amounts of risk without the corresponding responsibility. This study argues that only the personalisation of risk management – getting closer to it and smarter about it – will bring about real, last-ing recovery. Among the report's recommendations are that, as part of the recovery, banks must develop high-quality information, and avoid situations where the decision maker is too far removed from the action to feel responsible. By contrast, the report cites the highly cohesive and responsive top management team at JP Morgan Chase, whose closeness allowed them to foresee problems in the markets as early as

1 www.aimresearch.org 21 September 2009

2006 and to reduce their exposure to subprime mortgages, thereby allowing them to escape the financial crisis largely unscathed. Only when bureaucracy is dead can the economy really come alive.

Urgently, as soon as you can, you need to brainstorm with your colleagues to determine, with precision and focus, what parts of your bureaucracy can be attacked, and where you can further cut costs linked to this bureaucracy. If you must cut, cut with a reason; make this your objective. Look afresh at the structures and layers you take for granted, think about how they may actually be hindering what you do. This is inevitably going to be a difficult and painful task, but the consequences of doing nothing at all are certain to be far worse.

The polar opposite of bureaucracy is empowerment. Empowerment, however, is one of the most misunderstood and misused words in all business language. Conventionally, empowerment is perceived as being about giving something to someone. It is not. Rather, it is about taking something away. It is about taking fear and bureaucracy out of the decision-making process. The freedom that people think of as empowerment will emerge from this taking away. Freedom is nothing but freedom from fear, freedom to make decisions unconstrained by worrying about the bureaucratic consequences, and to move the business forward by doing all these things. What are you doing to take away the barriers to freedom, thereby encouraging the people who work with you and for you to make their own decisions more often?

Perhaps the most famous example in recent years of how a company's original business model successfully cut out bureaucracy and the barriers between it and its customers, is Dell computers. 'From the beginning,' Michael Dell has said, 'I was always thinking "what's the most efficient way to accomplish this?"' Dell believed close-

Getting close to your customers is not about a one-night stand

ness to the customer was the answer, and in the early days he was able to eliminate most instances of bureaucracy before they arose. One beautiful example of how the company got closer and smarter was that he made his sales reps assemble their own computers. He doesn't doubt, he says, that this was highly unpopular, but he believes that it gave the people on the front line of selling Dell's products an intimate understanding of what the average customer would go through. They could then sell and support the products to overcome these challenges by assisting customers to make informed decisions about what to buy. When Michael Dell returned to his company as CEO in 2007, as a result of poor performance in the years since he had stepped down, he announced in an email to staff that the company had a 'new enemy: bureaucracy'. He went so far as to call this the number one issue at Dell, believing that it had crept in and was sucking the energy and vibrancy away from the successful company he had always operated. To make his promise real, in the years that he has been back at the company, Dell has stripped away layers of redundant management bureaucracy, culling nearly half of his direct reports. Though the company is still going through some pretty tough times, so far Dell's initiatives seem to be producing the reinvigorating results hoped for.

At a far more local level in the UK, the very successful and well-known high street shoe repair chain Timpson has achieved some quite astounding results by cutting out bureaucracy and freeing up staff to make decisions on their own. The Timpson chain is ubiquitous on shopping streets all over the UK, having expanded from its original shoe repair base. Now also they cut keys, mend watches, engrave plaques, and create house signs. Whenever Timpson takes over a rival chain, the first thing it does is to remove the Electronic Point of Sale systems on which most high-street businesses operate. This might seem like a technologically reactionary move. Indeed, when they do this, many employees seem wary, not sure how they will be measured, or what they can do without the security of the EPOS system. Instead, Timpson's publishes a set of guide prices, but gives managers the responsibility and flexibility to decide for themselves what price they will be charging – this means that they have the freedom not to charge for a simple job, such as fixing a watch strap, but can charge more for jobs that prove longer and more complex. Timpson's staff are free to do favours for their customers, and to practise small kindnesses such as allowing someone who doesn't have the right money on them to bring it into the shop later. Rather than adhering to strict, centrally-controlled targets, each shop is measured on just one big target: how much revenue it brings in each week. The resulting closeness to customers, and lasting relationships with them, is indeed a great success story.

Darwin of course was proven right. Survival is all about adaptability. Successful relationships, in your business and in your personal life, are about adaptability. Killing bureaucracy will make your business more adaptable. Killing bureaucracy will get you closer to customers. Getting closer to customers will make you smarter in delivering what they need right now, not what they needed several years ago. You are not smart if you believe the recession changed little. Get smart and get ready to focus on what really matters to people in the post-recession era. Before you push the re-start button as the recession fades into memory, pay attention to these simple messages. All of these things need to be part of the Common Purpose that unites and inspires the thinking and, more importantly, the actions of you and your colleagues. It is all part of the revolution.

Chapter 6

Building a Common Purpose

L ike all revolutions, the Relationship Revolution is about change and about action. You have a choice: you can fantasise about what was, what might have been, what could have been – or you can choose to be free of denial, nostalgia and arrogance and decide that decisive action is indeed necessary at this defining moment. Great leadership is about both the vision to see and the courage to take action. Like any other revolution, success will depend on the commitment, solidarity, sheer drive and consistent actions of the people who work with you and for you, fighting to bring about the necessary changes to survive in the post-recession era. More important than anything else, however, is focus. Success is not about size, it is about focus: a clear focus, a sustained focus, a focus that is applicable to everyone, everywhere in your organisation regardless of hierarchy or geography. It is about as many people as possible within your enterprise working together towards a Common Purpose.

I have long believed that organisations never really change. Instead, people change. They change their focus. They change what they believe is important to ensure their success and survival. They change their actions. They provide or withdraw their support accordingly. They then influence like-minded people who together build the necessary critical mass to make change inevitable. They recruit and reward and retain people to their cause based on a renewed Common Purpose. This is how revolutions, small and big alike, in politics and in business, begin and spread. Change begins with the individual – always. Change begins with you.

People working together driven by a Common Purpose may be as crucial to your business, in the short and the long term, as your cash position. The only difference is that you can count the latter and not the former. The fact that you cannot quantify Common Purpose only makes it that much more important to remain constantly vigilant about whether it is present, about whether it is embedded deep in your organisation, about whether it is tangibly alive to the majority of your colleagues. There are no spreadsheets or formulas to help you measure this, which is why it may be the ultimate challenge to anyone in a leadership role of any kind anywhere in the world. If your quest is to achieve greatness, understand that greatness is impossible to achieve and even harder to sustain without a defined, agreed-upon, identifiable, and constantly communicated Common Purpose.

I am sure that it is abundantly clear to everyone reading this book that I believe the most important Common Purpose today is focusing on the reality that customer relationships will be *the* dominant factor in determining success in the post-recession era. In fact, this has been my belief throughout my entire career – consistently throughout the last 35 years. Has there ever been a time, ever, when business success was not predicated upon the building and maintenance of customer relationships? Every loyalty programme in the world was created in recognition of this reality.

Think of the challenges of building a Common Purpose today when the workplaces of the world are, to a remarkable extent, global, mobile, temporary, outsourced, off-shore, part-time, at home, 24/7 and, recently, depleted of millions and millions of workers. How do you 'build' something in this environment that helps people to focus on a Common Purpose? What kind of architect, and architecture, is required for this kind of building activity? Do you have the patience – the stomach – to take the first steps to put these building blocks in place? Do you understand the rewards of doing so? Do you understand the opportunity costs of not contemplating this action? Is the building of a Common Purpose on your list of the five most important actions to consider to ensure you survive this recession?

On this topic I speak from having 'done the job'. I was privileged to have spent ten years at British Airways during their 'glory days', when they were not only the most profitable airline in the world but also a customer service

Organisations never really change. Instead, people change

icon. I did not begin the remarkable cultural and financial transformation of the airline, only helped to sustain it during a particular moment in time. Many others, too numerous to mention, were far more responsible than I was in the building of a hugely successful global airline, in an industry where it is a miracle that any company can make a profit.

In the late 1970s and early 1980s, British Airways was a government-owned, bloated, bureaucratic and bankrupt company. When I joined in 1989 the company had already undergone a remarkable transformation under the leadership of Colin Marshall and John King. It became the 'World's Favourite Airline' by moving from an operations-led company to a market-led one, totally obsessed with customer relationships and the service that was provided. Today, with BA's woes in the news almost daily, this may seem difficult to remember. But for more than a decade, from the late 1980s until around the start of the millennium, this obsession with customer relationships helped BA to become not only the most profitable airline in the world – on a cumulative basis – but more than that, a constant case study of how a company can successfully sustain profitability by building a Common Purpose focused on building and maintaining customer relationships.

See training as an investment, not a cost

My involvement in all this was with a programme called 'Winning for Customers', the fourth in a decade-long series of corporate awareness programmes that began with the world famous and much copied 'Putting People First'. In two years, between 1992 and 1994, 'Winning for Customers' was attended by nearly 55,000 British Airways employees. One hundred people from all over the world would gather each day in London to focus together on one core issue: the role that *everyone* had in the building and maintenance of customer relationships regardless of where they worked in the company. This programme was organised to make customer loyalty part of everyone's job – to make it the Common Purpose and to explain the economic necessity of retaining customers. The key messages of the programme were:

- *deliver* (be obsessed with delivering great service all the time);
- *recover* (quickly take responsibility and try to put things right when something has gone wrong); and
- *retain* (success for everyone would be linked to retaining loyal customers).

To this day, 'Winning for Customers' still stands out as an unique example of a company deciding that, if customer loyalty was to become a reality, *everyone had to own it*: pilots, caterers, engineers, reservationists, cabin crew, cleaners, drivers – every single person had to understand the economics of customer loyalty and their individual role in making it happen. The potential lifetime value latent in every customer relationship was creatively brought to the attention of nearly every single person in the company during this three-year programme.

'Winning for Customers' worked across hierarchies and across geographies too. People came from all parts of the business, and all parts of the world, to attend these sessions. They came from Argentina and Japan, from Sri Lanka and the Bahamas, from Botswana and America, reflecting BA's status as a truly global company. The mere fact of communicating to employees that the company cared enough about them, and their development, to go to such lengths as to bring them to London for this event, was a major factor in the triumph of the programme.

'Winning for Customers' may be an extreme example of how far a company would go to build a Common Purpose, but representatives of companies from outside of British Airways, and outside of the airline industry, came from all over the world to study this model of a corporate awareness programme, seeing it as the very best example they could find of how an enterprise could endeavour to focus an entire workforce on a single economic principle that would benefit their business as a result. Many believe that 'Winning for Customers' was the most successful corporate awareness programme ever conducted in Europe. This kind of success should reinforce the idea that events like this are an investment, and not just a cost.

Yet this is also a cautionary tale. In recent years, BA has often been thought of as anything but a corporate success story. The press is now full of fresh bad news about poor industrial relations, meals not being included on short-haul flights and cabin crew numbers being reduced. This seems like a race to the bottom of the market, and a desire to compete on price with the budget airlines, rather than to compete on the basis of the building and maintaining of customer relationships to create Value for Life by providing world-class customer service. This is another big lesson about the building of a Common Purpose: you have never done it completely and the quest never ends. As a leader, you can never sit back and think that it's been achieved. Building a Common Purpose is a constant quest, where your ability to adapt is more important than how smart you are, and where you must resist arrogance and/or denial. No revolution can rest on its laurels.

Much of this book has been focused on the ubiquitous search for value in the post-recession era. Value is at the forefront of everyone's mind: customers looking for value, and you and

No revolution can rest on its laurels

your colleagues looking to create value in the running of your enterprise. Now is the time to make the link between this universal search for value and the organisational values that define the true heart and character of your business. After the comprehensive collapse of trust and confidence as a result of this recession, has there ever been a time when company values have been more important than they are today? The values of a company are its DNA, its genetic code. They may say more about who you are and what you stand for than any of your other stated intentions. Values are the new rule book that all of your colleagues should always carry in their head and in their heart. When making any kind of decision, people simply need to ask themselves: is this in line with the values of the company? How much financial misery could have been avoided in the past two years if this was a common practice? In the context of globalisation, which you should remind yourself has not disappeared as a result of this recession, the values of the company are its moral compass.

At the heart of the Relationship Revolution will be a requirement for ethical leadership

There exists an almost mandatory obligation to align company values with the individual values of the people who work there. Study after study has shown that the biggest reason people fail in their jobs has little to do with being lazy, ignorant or even morally corrupt. They fail because their personal values were obtuse to the values of the organisation. What are you doing to measure and better understand this alignment when you are hiring someone to join your company or evaluating someone already there? Whose responsibility is it? Is there a collective responsibility to get this right? What are the opportunity costs of getting this wrong? How disruptive and potentially disastrous is it to have even a small minority of your perceived key employees who choose to operate and make decisions that are not aligned to the values of the organisation? When written, much of the history of the recent global financial meltdown will, I predict, focus on this disparity.

After my time at BA, I spent the final three years of my corporate life at Airmiles, the British Airways wholly-owned loyalty management company. When the 'Winning for Customers' programme concluded, I joined Airmiles as Director of Customer Service. It was a perfect segue into a pure loyalty environment, and in many ways the experience served to crystallise my views on what Value for Life really means. After 18 months as Director of Customer Service, I became Director of People and Culture, the first person in Europe to ever have this role and title in any organisation. This was an overt attempt to redefine the relevance of HR as a function. In that role, I was able to live out my deeply-held belief that HR and customer service aren't different things at all – they exist on a continuum, and the ability to create value through customer relationships is directly linked to who you recruit, how you reward, why you retain, and the fundamental need to align peoples' actions to the values of the company.

How serious were we at Airmiles when trying to determine the alignment of company values? Consider our process of Trinity Interviews. This was the final step in the recruitment process for anyone at supervisor level or above who was attempting to join the organisation. They were called Trinity Interviews because they always involved three directors of the company, often including the CEO, interviewing every candidate for the very final approval to hire. The sole objective in these interviews was not to test for experience, intelligence or aptitude, but to try and ascertain if that person was truly aligned with the stated values of the organisation. If even one of the three directors felt that there wasn't a values match, the rule was that we wouldn't hire. We felt it was that important an issue. However talented, experienced and impressive someone was, if we felt that they couldn't connect with the company's values, they were rejected. An imperfect science? A purely subjective measurement? A brutal final hurdle? Perhaps. Yet these Trinity Interviews, I still believe, were the most tangible and serious statement attesting to the importance of company values I have ever encountered in my entire career, and a way to bring another dimension to what is meant by focusing on a Common Purpose.

Values in an organisation can be validated in many ways. They can and must sometimes be adapted, as the objectives of the organisation are adapted to meet new economic realities – after all, Common Purpose is a moving target. In 2007, for instance, Nokia announced new company values which were the result of a bottom-up process involving thousands of their employees. The Nokia new values unveiled at that time were:

- Achieving Together
- Engaging You
- Passion for Innovation
- Very Human

These values emerged from 16 Nokia Way internal events attended by nearly 2000 employees. Over 100 people attended each of these events, representing various personnel groups from different countries and different competencies. These discussions were perhaps unique in their determination to include as many people as possible in the search for company values to commit and to work by. Representative hierarchies and geographies from all over the world participated, in what many now consider to be a classic example of inclusiveness when building a Common Purpose in a global enterprise as based on company values.

What are your company values? Are they abstract or are they in some way tangible? Can the majority of your colleagues, at every hierarchy and everywhere in the world, quickly say what they are? Are they the rule book by which people judge their actions? The values of a company and/ or its Common Purpose need to be *unambiguous*. They need to be repeated. They need to be ring-fenced. They need to be part of the criteria by which the performance of every individual is judged. They need to be part of the recruitment process. They need to be central and present and made to be real. They can never be delegated, any more than trust can be delegated. Under what circumstances would you delegate trust? Under what circumstances would you delegate values? Under what circumstances would you delegate building a Common Purpose?

In a world where transparency is now a certain requirement, and where there is nowhere to hide any longer, the ethics of an organisation form another integral component of the Common Purpose. The recent list of ethical casualties is too long and, indeed, too painful, to repeat here. It should simply be understood that your ethics will determine your fate, the fate of your company and the fate of your career. You should not have a Director of Ethics in your organisation, as that serves to wrongly assign ethics to a specific department. Ethical behaviour is the platform on which any Common Purpose must be constructed, and is the responsibility of every single individual.

At the heart of the Relationship Revolution will be a requirement for ethical leadership. Such leadership will need to build a Company of Citizens in an atmosphere of dignity and trust throughout the organisation; building a new social architecture as required by this recession where values and character and Common Purpose are centre stage. These things can never simply be contracted out, as so much else has been during recent times as a cost-savings exercise. Doing so jeopardises all of your goals, reduces your credibility and sells your soul. Without a distinct and defined Common Purpose, supported by clearly-understood company values, openly communicated inside and outside your organisation, you will fail to attract talented people in the future, you will lose many of your most talented people and your race to the bottom will be accelerated.

Chapter 7

Talent, as Precious as Oil

What is most valuable is what is most rare: gold, diamonds, silver, rubies, platinum, emeralds, sapphires – and oil. No economy in the world is fully dependent on precious gems and metals. Every economy in the world is utterly dependent on oil. Every economy and every government and every business in the world, including yours, is fully dependent on talent. It is rare, it is precious, it is scarce, and it is the single most important element in your ability to succeed in the post-recession era and beyond.

The successful execution of everything in this book is dependent on the actions of the people who work with you and for you: their motivation, their focus, their passion, their ability to adapt. New wealth and value will come from the innovation and creativity of your most talented people, given the freedom to realise their full potential, and not from squeezing the last bit of efficiency out of the old way of doing things. Cut, cut, cut, you may have done in the past several years in order to survive, but those steps alone will not be the building blocks to sustain lifetime value in your most important customer relationships. Only the actions of your most talented people, driven by a Common Purpose, obsessed and totally focused on the Relationship Revolution, will deliver the value you are seeking as your legacy.

I believe there is never a shortage of talent – never! There is only a shortage of great companies that the best people want to work for. Are you one of those companies? Are you a magnet for talent? This is the single most important question a Chief Executive can ask of an HR Director: are we a magnet for talent? If not, why not? It must be asked over and over and over again. HR as a function continues to suffer from an inferiority complex, as a result of focusing on the wrong things for too many years. Much of what HR had focused on in the past 20 years has now been contracted out owing to the fact it was not relevant to core business strategy.

There is never a shortage of talent, only a shortage of great companies that the best people want to work for

Is anything *more* relevant than talent management? What could be more relevant than recruiting, rewarding and retaining the right people for the right length of time. What could be more relevant than creating a culture and environment where talented people have the freedom to realise their full potential.

How often in the past have you heard various Chief Executives say: 'People are our most important asset'? How often did you think, and perhaps know, they did not actually believe that statement, or certainly did not act like they believed that statement? What damage has been done as a result? Do a quick trawl of company websites and HR literature, and count up how many times the phrase, or others like it, are used. How often is this promise made real in the way that companies treat their people on a daily, weekly and yearly basis? My experience, and I'm guessing yours too, is a tiny fraction of the amount of times that it's said. This phrase has become so ingrained in the corporate lexicon that it's become almost meaningless. If you say it to your employees, do they just sigh and roll their eyes, or do they actually believe it? Some advice: do not say it unless your actions support it. Otherwise you look like a fool.

You need to close the Promise Gap not just with your customers, but with your employees as well. Let's come back to the analogy of business life akin to that of a personal relationship. Is it OK to say 'I love you' and not mean it, over and over and over again, just because you think you ought to? Most people would think not. In that case, why are so many powerful people so willing to make such a dramatic pronouncement to their staff about their intrinsic importance as an asset to the company. Just because they think they ought to, or because all their competitors are saying it, without really believing it? If you do this, you're creating a Promise Gap with your staff, perhaps even more dangerous than between you and your customers.

If you believe that customer relationships will be *the* dominant factor in determining success in the post-recession era, and these relationships will create Unique Value in an age where *everyone* is looking for value, then the successful execution of all this comes down to aligning your Talent Plan with your Business Plan. Of course you have a Business Plan, reviewed and perhaps adjusted every quarter of the business year. Do you also have a Talent Plan that is issued as often as your Business Plans and align with them accordingly? If not, why not? The biggest waste of time and money in any business is when talent and strategy are not aligned. Talent is a strategic priority. Is it in your company? If so, how is it made tangible? Would your staff agree? Whose vote counts more?

The convergence of people, customers and culture has been a burning passion right through my career. During my time at Airmiles, I pioneered the first comprehensive corporate mentoring model in Europe, not just for the people at the top, but everyone from the supervisors right up to directors. Everyone had a personal mentor. Everyone had a requirement to meet with their mentor a specific number of times per month. This process was born from my passionate belief that talent was indeed a strategic priority, and every effort had to be made to align talent with strategy by giving people time to focus, with someone who was not their boss, on the most important issues they were confronting. This robust mentoring programme was built around a simple premise:

1. Helping people to realise the *challenges* they faced.
2. Helping people to realise the *choices* they had.
3. Helping people to realise the *consequences* of their choices and their actions.

This, I believe, is one fundamental way of making the most of the talent in your organisation and making the people feel valued. This kind of investment of both time and capital makes it demonstrably clear that people may indeed be the most important asset in the company.

Hire the most talented people you can afford. Nurture them. Feed them. Invest in them. Watch them grow. Set them free. When people choose to stay, why do they stay? Rather than being obsessed solely with exit interviews and why people leave your company, are you equally obsessed as to why your most talented people decide to remain?

Of course people stay with and leave companies for many different reasons. Survey after survey has proven that people now rarely stay or leave just because of what they are paid. Similarly, your talented people are also likely to be your least inert people – they're almost certainly not the ones biding their time because they can't be bothered to look for something better, or because they doubt that anyone else would have them. The reasons to stay may have changed dramatically in the past several years and may now have much to do with information, choice, power and control. Sound familiar? The symmetrical needs of both your most talented people *and* your most loyal customers should be apparent.

The best organisations to work in, for the most talented people, have three inherent common characteristics:

1. Open Communication – 'I know what's going on'
2. Open Contribution – 'I know I can make a difference'
3. Open Opportunity – 'I know I can advance'

Communicate, Collaborate and Advance. Your talented employees want to do exactly the same things as your most loyal customers, only more so. After all, for your customers, their engagement with you and your products may only take place every week, or every couple of months. For your employees, their engagement with you is likely to make up as much as half of their waking hours. How much more demanding does that mean they're going to be? What are you doing to service these demands?

The current generation of workers, like the current generation of customers, is used to communicating all the time, and accepts social networking and constant conversation as a way of life. Just as you need to be discovering in real-time, all the time, what your customers are saying about you, your company, your products, your service, your culture, your values – and whilst you engage with them directly to adapt and create value – you also need to think about your internal social networks and what the people who work with you and for you are saying. Are you ignoring this, or pretending that it's not happening, or are you there, engaging with them, adapting, responding, and encouraging their communication and participation? Just like you should be doing with your customers – in real-time, all the time – to help build and maintain relationships and therefore the value in the company.

In both their personal and professional lives, workers in the future will be used to collaboration as being normal not exceptional. If you don't give your people the ability to collaborate and contribute across boundaries, divisions, hierarchy and geography, they will choose to go elsewhere. It's that important and it's that simple. Do not be fooled into thinking that, as a result of the recession, the mobility of your most talented people

The biggest waste of time and money is when talent and strategy are not aligned

has disappeared. If you do not have a culture that celebrates the sharing of ideas, you are doomed.

Ideas are the very lifeblood of talent. In essence, they are what make talented people talented. Very talented people have the vision to see, and also the courage to take action. The freedom you give them to communicate, collaborate and participate will determine their ability to succeed. Therefore, an obsession with killing bureaucracy matters just as much, if not more, to the people inside your organisation as it does to your customers. Hiring talented people today and placing them inside an anachronistic environment full of bureaucracy is almost criminal. It may be the easiest way for you to waste time and money, because they will soon leave. As with customers, in the post-recession era there will be nowhere to hide from angry, frustrated and cynical staff. Broken promises and hollow pronouncements are certain to damage the only tool you have for engaging and keeping your best talent, your credibility. These angry, frustrated, cynical and very talented people will also be telling people in their social networks (often other very talented people) that the working environment and culture of your company is dreadful…or worse.

People realise their greatest success when they are passionate about what they do

Everything in the way you recruit, retain and reward talent, like the way you think about your relationships with your customers, has been seismically influenced by the once-in-a-generation effects of global downturn and recession. Prior to the recession, the talk of a 'war for talent' had been popular in business discourse for several years. The original research for the study 'The War for Talent' was conducted by McKinsey in 1997. It identified the key demographic trends: the looming retirement of the Baby Boomer generation, coupled with declining populations in the developed world (and therefore a dearth of young workers entering the workplace), meant that finding, motivating and retaining capable workers was likely to be one of the greatest challenges faced by global business in the decades ahead. Basically, the McKinsey report made it abundantly clear that talent was a ticking time bomb for twenty-first-century business. In 2006, a follow-up survey suggested that business leaders still considered finding appropriate talent as the single biggest managerial challenge. As the recession erupted, altering the economic landscape to an almost unprecedented degree, many seemed to feel that talent would move to the back burner. As unemployment reached over 10% of the workforce in America, with developed countries all over the world displaying similar figures, suddenly talent appeared to be a worry which belonged in happier times. With economic conditions forcing some of the most established and formerly successful companies to lay off some of their best people, it seemed that suddenly talent would be abundant rather than scarce, and the scales would swing, creating an employer's market again.

This is and isn't true. Surviving through the challenges of the recession has been all about knowing how to cut costs without cutting your throat. Do you know if you have cut too much of your best talent? How do you know? What measurements do you employ to determine this? Even if you have avoided falling into this trap, many of your competitors almost certainly have not. The recession has afforded nimble, savvy companies everywhere the opportunity to pick up their competitors' talent (and with it, much of their competitors' knowledge and experience). There are now great people floating around the jobs market, in a way that a couple of years earlier you could only have dreamed of. Do you know who they are, or where they are, and what they want? *Now is the time* to be certain you are a magnet for talent, to ensure that you are attracting the best people while you can, to ensure the Relationship Revolution exists both inside and outside your company.

The talent of the people you recruit must be matched by their passion for what they are recruited to do. If not, either do not hire them or find them a role in which they really will work with passion. When you're hiring, passion may be *the* most important, and yet perhaps the most elusive, thing to measure. You are being lazy if you get lured into the trap of hiring a very talented person without attempting to measure their passion for the role for which they are being hired. Not to do so is to waste resources on a potentially enormous scale. People realise their greatest success when they're deeply passionate about what they do.

You must target and attract potential talented employees in almost the same way as you try to target and attract potential lifetime customers. A McKinsey Quarterly Report in 2008 argued that you must focus deeply on your 'value proposition' whilst trying to win the War for Talent. This value proposition, in both scenarios, is in many ways focused on your brand value as a company, and what it stands for. How attractive is your company brand to the most talented people you are trying to attract? You need to know what works for the differing needs and demands of those in Generation Y as well as Generation X. You need to know whether you are able to attract older workers, still full of wisdom and experience, for whom the word retirement may suggest little that is desirable. You may even need to be able to attract those from well beyond your national borders, to get the best talent from emerging markets. Remember, getting closer makes you smarter. Smarter then makes you ready for the Relationship Revolution already under way amongst your current employees, your future employees and your customers.

In his many prescient works of management theory, the great writer and philosopher Charles Handy, perhaps the most profoundly accurate judge of trends relating to work and organisations of the last century, was the first to describe the emerging trend towards *Talent only soars when it's set free* portfolio careers. In the future, he argued, companies would hire people as would a Hollywood Studio for a film, matching the right person for the right job for the right length of time – project to project to project. I said at the start of this chapter that talent was as precious, and as much of an economic necessity, as oil. Perhaps then it is no coincidence that Handy began his career as an employee of the Royal Dutch Shell oil company.

Oil has made many people very rich. I have asked the following questions to many audiences when doing speeches in the Gulf: 'Oil has made you rich, but will talent keep you rich in the future?' 'Is there a "Talent Pipeline" in your company?' You might consider answering some of these questions as well, whether you have been made rich by oil or not.

Fundamentally, focusing on talent is about aiming high. Citizens and customers alike are pushing all the time for political and economic behaviour that aims higher. The belief in progress is ingrained deeply in the human psyche. If you can't match this, you'll only be left behind by companies who are more prescient, more active, more far-sighted, more adaptable and more talented themselves. In the course of my career, I've found that talent only soars when it's set free. Think about the best boss you ever had. I'll predict that it is most likely the person who gave you the most freedom to realise your full potential. Now think: are you that kind of boss to your people right now? If not, why not? That person should be your role model, and your goal must be to help your people to realise their full potential.

Perhaps the most successful advocate and promoter of talent in recent times is also renowned as one of the toughest, most feared and respected businessmen of the last century – Jack Welch, the legendary former Chairman and CEO of General Electric. Famously, during his tenure at GE, Welch would advocate replacing the 'bottom' ten per cent of his managers every year, those who were underperforming or simply no longer fitted with the culture and values of GE. This might sound counter-intuitive, but it's hard to argue with the success that GE had under Welch's leadership. As he asked in his book *Winning*, which focused almost exclusively on talent management: 'is aiming to cut 10% every year cruel and Darwinian, or is it in fact fair and effective?' Welch goes on to explain his philosophy:

> 'Companies win when their managers *make a clear and meaningful distinction* between top and bottom performing businesses and people, when they cultivate the strong and cull out the weak in an honest and open manner.'

Welch also ruthlessly broke down the layers of hierarchy and bureaucracy at GE, allowing everyone a better opportunity to make their fullest contribution. During his tenure, he invested a remarkable amount of time visiting the company's world-famous training centre at Croton-on-Hudson, talking face to face with new executives, allowing them to question him, listening and pushing right back. This informality and closeness, Welch argued, made him smarter. He suggested that near the end of his career at GE he dedicated close to 50 per cent of his time as CEO to issues related to talent. That close. That smart. That ready to succeed.

Jack Welch left an astonishing legacy at GE. He is credited with having created $57 billion of value during his years leading the company. Legacy is something which preoccupies almost all successful business leaders. Your legacy will have little to do with how rich you personally become. It will rest on the success of your business in the years after you leave, which more than anything else has to do with the talent that you're bringing in right now. The Relationship Revolution is at hand – it's talented people who will make it a success.

Chapter 8

The Virtuoso Way:
How One-to-One Relationships
Revolutionised Luxury Travel

The challenges presented to us by the Relationship Revolution may seem daunting; even, at times, overwhelming. To get *really* close to your customers, to build relationships based on trust, to hand over power, information and control, and to build a business based on service and talent, takes bold vision, great skill and enormous courage. Do you have what it takes to do all this?

The good news from the barricades of the revolution is that *it can be done.* In my own experience, I've seen, worked with and given speeches to companies that have achieved historic things by being part of the Relationship Revolution before it was forced upon them. I'd like to focus on one such company, Virtuoso. With headquarters in Ft Worth, Texas, the Virtuoso network is the United States' largest seller of luxury leisure travel, with annual sales of more than $5.2 billion. How have they done all this? They are a company from an industry I know very well indeed – the travel sector – an industry which in the last three decades has been traumatised by cataclysmic change. Yet this company is a remarkable success story of how the creation of Unique Value, by focusing on one-to-one personal relationships, can revolutionise an entire industry and can triumph. They saw the future before the competition – and they got there first!

This story commences over 30 years ago, when the real boom in travel agencies began with the 1977 deregulation of the airline industry in America. As a result of this deregulation, fares became infinitely more complex, with a dizzying array of prices and a plethora of arcane booking codes. The only way that airlines could manage this complexity effectively was to use travel agencies for ticket reservations and the supporting customer service, having calculated that agency commission as a cost of sales and distribution was more economical than providing these services directly. Thirty years on, this decision to outsource distribution, and the failure to associate that distribution with customer relationships, is arguably a defining moment for the challenges that continue to face the travel industry today. The airlines' great mistake was to fall into the trap of confusing value with price. They are still struggling to emerge.

In the mid 1990s, things got even worse when the airlines, again seeking to control costs, dropped travel agency commissions from 10% to 5% – another relationship severed by the idea that the value in relationships can be measured immediately in dollars and cents. After 9/11, and all the horror it brought for the travel industry, traditional commissions to travel agencies disappeared altogether. Of the agencies that remain, most charge the clients a booking fee to handle airline reservations that the client could do themselves for no more than the cost of a broadband connection. Why then do intermediaries account for around half of all ticket sales? Quite simply, clients would rather pay a fee for service than deal directly with the airlines. What does that tell you about the relationship between the airline industry and its customers?

The airlines were not alone in deciding to target travel agencies and the cost of distribution in the $6 trillion world-wide travel industry. Bill Gates and Microsoft opened Expedia in 1995, and changed forever the way people would make travel reservations. When the change came, it came fast. In 1996, Microsoft ran its first full page advert in the *Wall Street Journal*, urging customers to access 'the same reservation system' that travel agents used, all from the comfort of their own desk. By March 1997, Expedia reported that it had booked $1 million of travel reservations in a seven-day period. Airline bookings represented 80% of this volume. By January 2002, the internet accounted for 14.4% of all travel bookings. Analysts sounded the death knell for the bricks-and-mortar travel agency.

Be part of the Relationship Revolution before it is forced on you

It really did seem like a perfect storm. A steep decline in customer demand following 9/11; an oversupply of inventory – brought to market in the anticipation of an influx of affluent, retiring baby-boomers – which suppliers were now forced to fill at almost any price; and the fast, convenient, price-based, borderless world of the internet. Only woe awaits any middle man in these circumstances.

So how has the Virtuoso network of travel agencies (350 world-wide, with 6000 travel advisors, supported by 1600 travel suppliers), in the midst of this maelstrom of fundamental structural change to the travel industry, not only survived but grown to become an industry icon?

In October 1988, a fortuitous mix of individuals came together: an industry veteran, Jesse Upchurch; a young, inspiring visionary, Matthew Upchurch; a well-regarded travel industry expert, Walter Jost, who had previously led a group of travel agencies under the umbrella organisation called Allied Travel; and an adroit marketer and businesswoman, Kristi Jones. The problem they wanted to solve was how could clients receive travel information at their own 'speed of life'. Seven years before the launch of Expedia, these four proposed to a small group of sceptical travel agency owners a new approach to selling luxury travel. The idea was to create a lifestyle magazine that featured the departures of key travel suppliers in an editorial format, customised for each agency and direct-mailed to the client's home.

Virtuoso championed the concept of 'return on life'

The idea took hold. *Voyage* magazine, one of the world's first 'magalogues', was an innovation that simplified the lives of travel agents and travel suppliers by distributing travel offers directly to customers at their individual 'speed of life', which in the late 1980s was print. In 1988, the distribution of information was a key problem facing both luxury travel suppliers, who would spend tens of thousands of dollars creating product brochures, and travel agencies then faced with the daunting task of selective distribution of this information to the right clients. At that time, 35,000 mainly independently-owned travel agencies were the primary source of sales for cruises, luxury tours, and independent foreign itineraries. How then to organise the best interests of the key stakeholders (travel agencies, travel suppliers and, of course, their customers) in this disparate yet burgeoning commercial arena? The genesis of this case study began as a co-operative; small, boutique travel agencies banded together in a New York City office and decided that the future of the industry was to form 'critical mass' by the building of relationships and the sharing of information. It was the beginning of a Relationship Revolution which changed this industry forever.

Today, that small, privately-held company has grown up to compete with giants in travel distribution: Expedia, Travelocity and American Express. The ultimate success of Virtuoso is based on their understanding that value lay not in the mechanics of distributing information, be that magalogues, direct-mail or computer screens, but in fostering the relationships represented in travel agencies' databases.

The travel agencies which formed the Virtuoso network had built their businesses one client at a time. Their success so far had lain in remembering their clients' anniversaries and birthdays, the ages of their children, their food preferences, what they thought of their last trip, what they dreamed of doing in their retirement. These travel agencies were not afraid to get *really* close to the customer. Such personal client knowledge was matched by real expertise about their suppliers.

These were agents who had travelled the world; they had established friendships with hoteliers, and they were able to call the presidents of cruise lines and ask favours, or help establish itineraries for tour operators. Put bluntly, they were very, very smart – by being very, very close to their customers.

Seven years later, many independent travel agencies faced disaster when Bill Gates, announcing the launch of Expedia, effectively told consumers to 'lose their travel agent's phone number'. Virtuoso was a lone voice in the wilderness, quoting T.S. Eliot's lines:

> 'Where is the wisdom we have lost in knowledge?
> Where is the knowledge we have lost in information?'[1]

Virtuoso accurately predicted that many consumers would find themselves lost in a jungle of information and choice. One person with a full-time job, and maybe kids and a house to look after, doesn't have time and doesn't want to spend all day, every day, surfing the web for their holiday. Instead, they were likely to want a compass to help them navigate and make informed choices. Virtuoso foresaw the role of travel agent transforming beyond that of a mere 'booker', to become a client consultant, advisor and advocate.

API Travel Consultants became Virtuoso in 2000. The name change reflected the change in their promise to the

---

1 Eliot, T.S. (1934) Choruses from *The Rock*, Faber & Faber, London.

customer. Virtuoso was designed to convey the network's ability and global reach, confirmed by the company's tagline: 'Specialists in the Art of Travel'. After that, it continued the company's precedent for opening up information. Virtuoso opened up the network of agents as a resource for consumer media, a forum which is always eager to know about new lifestyle trends and report on new, upcoming destinations. After all, more than 6000 advisors linked to Virtuoso travel the world each year, learning more and more about their destinations and the preferences of their clientele. Thus, the Virtuoso brand became synonymous throughout the US with upscale travel information and great sound bites, provided directly to reporters.

To consistently deliver on the customer promise of a more artisan kind of travel, the leadership at Virtuoso realised that they would have to invest significantly. They knew that their own Relationship Revolution was never going to happen on the cheap. The first of these significant investments was in technology. Perhaps surprisingly, even Expedia began as no more than a consumer interface to airline reservation screens. Realising that Expedia had perfected the do-it-yourself approach to mass travel, Virtuoso knew that they could only hope to win with something different. Matthew Upchurch, the CEO of Virtuoso says that 'all travel technology that currently exists deletes the human from the transaction'. Virtuoso aimed to use that technology to put the relationships back in. For that reason, Virtuoso developed the 'Composer' platform, to deliver on the company's promise that 'We Orchestrate Dreams'. The system is profile-centric, integrating client information, advocate recommendations, the latest, most relevant travel news, and a full range of travel options from over 1600 providers. All this information is delivered directly to the advisor to use in the service of their clients. In an age where everyone has sometimes felt deafened by the sheer noise of the internet, such ease and personalisation are hard to resist. Having recognised this at an early stage, Virtuoso and its network of advisors have been well-placed to exploit the new networking and communication channels opened up by the world of social media. By actively encouraging its advisors to operate Facebook pages and build up Twitter followings, Virtuoso has seen the benefits of connecting with clients over a deep, shared passion for travel.

To my mind, Virtuoso also understands that travel is a tool, not a solution. People are what make great service and great relationships really happen. Though we function in a high-tech, multitasking world where face-to-face contact has diminished, personal relationships are craved. Virtuoso believes that trustworthy, respectful relationships are the lifeblood of the industry's future. These relationships require time, substance, dialogue, exchange and understanding. To this end, Virtuoso has invested in professional development courses which it makes available free, or at very modest fees, to its sales agents. This has allowed the company to keep pace with the changing social profiles of travellers, from the social, amenable World War II generation to the self-directed Baby Boomers, and now Gen X and Gen Y. Only people can understand people, and build relationships that will meet their needs. Virtuoso's focus on people means that it has been able to attract some of the best young talent in the industry.

But what about that other crucial travel relationship, the one with the airlines, who are such a major supplier to any intermediary? As I noted earlier, right through the period of Virtuoso's growth, airlines had been cutting their commission to travel agents. Yet in these circumstances, as they deserted those agencies who failed to add value to the transaction, airlines were choosing to work with Virtuoso, in the knowledge that their network at the high-end of the industry could effectively fill up the front of most planes. Virtuoso solved this seeming problem by understanding just what relationships could do.

Virtuoso has been on the frontline in the battle against commoditisation

In 2008, for the first time this century, online travel experienced a decline in volume and customer satisfaction. More and more consumers reported frustration with the lack of personal service, or advice to guide them through the maze of online information. One recent survey showed that most online travel shoppers would prefer to work with a good travel advisor and would be willing to pay for the service provided.

Of course, for Virtuoso, as for almost any business that has operated in the past decade, the events of 9/11 and then the recent recession have posed very serious threats. Travel is a highly discretionary purchase; when supply suddenly exceeds demand, prompted either by global events or by consumer fears, prices and number of bookings drop to unsustainable levels. In both these events, Virtuoso's response has been to shift its message from one of sales to one of client support. In the immediate aftermath of 9/11, Virtuoso issued a statement arguing that 'boundaries divide and travel unites', making the case for the positive benefits of travel in what seemed like a troubled and frightening world. In 2009, in the teeth of one of the worst recessions in living memory, Virtuoso championed the concept of a 'return on life'. In a climate in which the value could be wiped off stocks and shares almost entirely in a matter of days, Virtuoso understood that its Unique Value was life value; very few people dispute that money spent on enriching travel experiences, shared with loved ones, is money wasted. Luxury, argues the leadership at Virtuoso, has been redefined in recent years. Words like 'bling' and 'ostentation' are most definitely out. Instead, what Virtuoso's client base wants is 'experiential,', 'timeless' and 'bespoke' travel, with the personal fulfilment that these words convey. In doing so, the upturn in Virtuoso's sales seems to suggest that it has been leading what may be a dramatic upturn in luxury travel.

For more than two decades, one event has captured the vision and Unique Value of the Virtuoso network: the Virtuoso

Travel Mart. The tagline for the event 'the power of one to one' really says it all. For four days, 3000 advisors, owners and suppliers come together to meet individually, to reinforce relationships and conduct business. In 2009, there were over 275,000 unique, one-to-one meetings, each establishing new relationships or strengthening old ones. I had the opportunity to do the keynote speech at this event in 2009, and was therefore able to experience this remarkable and unique feat of relationship building. Priceless indeed!

What I love about the story of Virtuoso is the way that relationships and an awareness of Unique Value lie at the very heart of everything they do. I find it hugely inspiring that, when faced with such daunting commercial challenges, the principles of the Relationship Revolution can guide you into less stormy waters and help you stay ahead of the crowd. Virtuoso was able to do this as a small, kitchen-table venture, and it's able to do it now as a true global leader and industry icon. Virtuoso has been on the front line of the battle against commoditisation in the full knowledge that elevating client satisfaction correlates with elevating profits. Realising that the only constant is change, Virtuoso has not only embraced the future, it has created it.

The story of Virtuoso is powerful, but its true potential lies in your ability to connect up the lessons here with your own battles in the Relationship Revolution. Could you face down change in the world this well? Do you know where you have to invest to build up the relationships that will carry you through? Are you quite this crystal clear about your markets, and where your Unique Value lies? The future is yours to create.

Epilogue

The Time is Now!

I t was never a career imperative of mine to write a book. When approached to consider writing this book, in the spring of 2009, it struck me that a defining moment in time was at hand. The global financial system had come close to catastrophe. So much of what people took for granted was under siege. Nothing focuses the mind more than fear, and many very successful friends and acquaintances were facing the most difficult time in their lives. Many were asking me the question: 'What will be the dominant factor in determining success in the post-recession era?' This book is a direct result of my attempt to answer that question.

I began the book with the following sentence: 'The urgency of the economic moment is clear.' My intent throughout the book was to bring a sense of urgency to help people focus on a core set of issues that I believed would determine their organisational survival. In my experience, it's always been about the customer. I do think it is impossible to refute that building and maintaining customer relationships is the key premise to commercial success of any kind. The idea of calling this book *The Relationship Revolution* was a simple attempt at capturing the clarity and the urgency of this. In an era when the search for value has been everybody's objective, it made total sense for the post-recession era reset button to be calibrated accordingly.

No one alone has all the answers. Always steer well clear of anyone who claims otherwise. I have, however, a lifetime of experience and have passionately focused on the issues which form the core premise of this book, and which inform everything I have argued here. I am sincerely hopeful that everyone who has taken the time to read this book takes from it one or two ideas that will help them to be more successful in the years ahead. In writing a book such as this, no objective has been more important.

Index